Confronting the Crisis of Engagement

Creating Focus and Resilience for Students, Staff, and Communities

Douglas Reeves

Nancy Frey

Douglas Fisher

A SAGE Publishing Company

FOR INFORMATION:

Corwin

A SAGE Company

2455 Teller Road

Thousand Oaks, California 91320

(800) 233-9936

www.corwin.com

SAGE Publications Ltd.

1 Oliver's Yard

55 City Road

London EC1Y 1SP

United Kingdom

SAGE Publications India Pvt. Ltd.

B 1/I 1 Mohan Cooperative Industrial Area

Mathura Road, New Delhi 110 044

India

SAGE Publications Asia-Pacific Pte. Ltd.

18 Cross Street #10-10/11/12

China Square Central

Singapore 048423

President: Mike Soules

Vice President and
  Editorial Director: Monica Eckman

Director and Publisher,
  Corwin Classroom: Lisa Luedeke

Associate Content Development
  Editor: Sarah Ross

Editorial Assistant: Nancy Chung

Production Editor: Melanie Birdsall

Typesetter: C&M Digitals (P) Ltd.

Proofreader: Theresa Kay

Cover Designer: Rose Storey

Marketing Manager: Allison Cottrell

Printed in the United States of America

ISBN 978-1-0718-9416-3

Library of Congress Control Number: 2022941686

This book is printed on acid-free paper.

22 23 24 25 26 10 9 8 7 6 5 4 3 2 1

Contents

Visit the companion website at
resources.corwin.com/crisisofengagement
for downloadable resources.

Introduction

The Engagement Imperative

A crisis of engagement has emerged because of the ongoing pandemic and its disruptions to all corners of society. Even among those who did not experience a direct loss, many students experienced *re-entry anxiety*, a term coined by mental health experts to describe the complex mixture of worries related to disease exposure, social unease after prolonged isolation from peers, and unfamiliarity with in-person schooling routines. The continuing wave of disruptions due to frequent quarantining and classroom closures further upend household routines related to getting up and out the door for school. It's difficult for families to build school-related momentum when a call can mean two weeks of the children in the house now staying home all day. Is it any wonder that we are seeing unprecedented levels of chronic absenteeism, a reluctance to participate in the classroom, and a reduction in expectations among teachers during an unsteady year?

Engagement and academic performance are inextricably linked. The challenges faced in classrooms are especially acute in high-poverty areas. In a national study of student performance before, during, and after school closures, Harvard professor Thomas Kane and colleagues found that learning losses were particularly acute in schools serving students from low-income families (Anderson 2022). Though Kane estimates that students are behind by 11 to 22 weeks of schooling, our anecdotal observations around the nation find many schools in which there is a full year or more of learning loss. Students in second and third grade do not yet know the alphabet; students in middle and high schools do not have the reading skills required to understand their science, social studies, and math textbooks. These are not challenges that will be resolved with Saturday school, after-school programs, homework packets, or study halls. These students need intensive support during the school day. The only solution is to rebuild student-teacher relationships so that the engagement that is essential to learning can be re-established.

As the world emerges from the global pandemic with interrupted formal education and many student absences, the norms of daily behavior, including interacting with peers and teachers, must be re-learned. Educators are worried about unfinished learning and desperately try to engage students in meaningful tasks that address learning needs (Kuhnfeld and Tarasawa 2020; World Bank 2021). As a result, teachers and school leaders face the daunting challenge of re-engaging students, academically and behaviorally, so that students have the opportunity to reach their potential and meet the challenges that a great educational environment can provide. But these aspirations will be a pipedream without a renewed commitment to what we believe is the foundation of learning and teaching: engagement. By *engagement,* we mean the mutually focused attention of students and teachers on curiosity, challenge, and learning. While much has been written about student engagement, we contend that this is only a part of the equation, for without deep engagement by teachers and school leaders, the expectation that students will be engaged is wishful thinking. In brief, if you expect students to be engaged, you must give teachers the time and space to engage with students. And if you expect teachers to be engaged, then leaders must be in a constant state of vigilance to focus the efforts of the entire school—every minute, every meeting, every initiative—on nothing other than the learning imperatives at hand.

. . . .

By *engagement*, we mean the mutually focused attention of students and teachers on curiosity, challenge, and learning.

. . . .

While the appeal of engagement may be obvious, we find that it is elusive because of the fragmentation that is prevalent in schools and districts. There is a global crisis in maintaining focus. The inability of students and adults to attend to an idea—especially new and challenging ideas essential for learning—for more than a few minutes at a time has impacted every facet of our lives (Hari 2022).

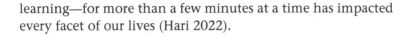

If we are to take the clarion call in this book for engagement seriously, it cannot be one more initiative.

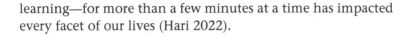

However, the failure of focus and the prevalence of initiative fatigue (Reeves 2021c) were pervasive long before the pandemic and the flood of federal dollars that were designed to help schools recover from it. Unfortunately, many of these funds brought programs that further scattered the attention of teachers, administrators, and students, and failed to provide the essential focus on learning that students desperately needed. This is not a new phenomenon, as federal educational aid programs in past decades, such as Race to the Top, yielded more dollars than sense. The evidence from a study of more than two thousand school plans reveals an inverse relationship between the number of initiatives and gains in student achievement (Reeves 2013). Therefore, if we are to take the clarion call in this book for engagement seriously, it cannot be one more initiative, announced with great solemnity in a school auditorium on top of the 23 other "top priorities" for the year. Engagement is the oxygen of learning. If you don't focus on that, teachers can only gasp for a few moments before all the other initiatives clamor for their attention. Therefore, this book is organized around the five Cs of engagement that, in turn, encompass so many other dimensions of schooling:

1. Connections

2. Conditions

3. Challenge

4. Control

5. Collaboration

We begin our exploration of engagement with **connections**— the essential relationships among students, teachers, and leaders that are the lifeblood of the school. Students don't come to school because they love algebra, but because they have deep connections with classmates and teachers. The essential nature of relationships is hardly unique to the schoolyard, as evidence from the organizational world reveals the power of emotional engagement for employees across industries and cultures (Edmondson 2018) and the destructive power of negative emotions in ruining work relationships (Porath and Pearson 2013). It is therefore baffling that the term "social and emotional learning" has become the object of criticism and abuse, as if only the parents and their fellow employees needed a decent and emotionally safe work environment, but their children should put their noses to the grindstone and get the work done. In Chapter 1 we explore connections not only in the classroom but also on the playground, athletic field, stage, and other opportunities for students to connect and develop relationships.

Chapter 2 focuses on the **conditions** that are necessary for engagement to thrive. As obvious as it sounds, students need to show up to school or to their learning environment if they are going to be able to engage. Further, students need to participate in the learning tasks. Finally, when teachers demonstrate high expectations for their learners, students are much more likely to engage. These conditions, combined with strong relationships, are foundational for engagement in learning.

Chapter 3 addresses the central paradox of engagement—*how do teachers simultaneously engage students with the encouragement and love that comes naturally to us, and* **challenge** *students to get out of their comfort zone and face disappointment and even the possibility of failure?* We challenge the conventional wisdom that engagement is antithetical to discomfort. In fact, we insist that part of our role as educators and leaders is to take children out of their comfort zone, endure the pain of mistakes, and create a fearless environment for error and the learning that it engenders. This has important implications for administrators who observe classrooms and who may inadvertently send the wrong message that an engaged classroom is one that reflects quiet and order (Gupta and Reeves 2021) rather than inquisitiveness, error, and a bit of chaos. There are great lessons to be learned from our music teachers and athletic coaches, who are able to provide honest feedback to students without the aid of a red pen or electronic grading systems: The note was sharp or flat. The basket was in or out. The goal was wide or in the net. But in the classroom, we too often temporize, encouraging work that is inadequate because we prefer the comfort of smiles and poor work over the discomfort of tears and corrected work.

Control is the subject of Chapter 4, in which we explore the ways in which students increase the ownership of their learning. The nexus between engagement and control may seem unusual, but it is vital. For educators to re-engage students in a post-pandemic world, we must design learning experiences that allow students to engage in self-regulation. Students need to know where they are going, select tools for their journey, and monitor their own progress. Each of these requires specific actions from teachers and opportunities to make mistakes along the way. But with practice and feedback, students can increase their ownership of learning, increasing their motivation and engagement along the way.

· ·

As difficult as collaboration may be, it is a key to engaging teachers and leaders and is more powerful as a motivator for them than other incentives.

· ·

In Chapter 5, we frame **collaboration** among students and teachers as an essential element of engagement. There is a lingering Emersonian ideal of self-reliance reflected in many classroom expectations in which "works independently" is a highly prized attribute. We examine critically the illusion of collaboration in which four students push desks together and pretend to collaborate, compared to the more challenging reality of collaboration in which each student must, with patience and perseverance, make independent contributions to the group. Collaboration is similarly difficult for adults. As difficult as collaboration may be, it is a key to engaging teachers and leaders and is more powerful as a motivator for them than other incentives that many educational systems use (Reeves 2018). If school and district leaders believe in collaboration, then they need to radically restructure their staff meetings, and give teachers real time for meaningful collaboration.

The book concludes with a chapter on **leadership essentials** for engagement. We are unstinting in our expectations that leaders change dramatically the primitive practices of staff meetings in which they make announcements to busy teachers. If we believe in engagement, then leaders must demonstrate that belief at every opportunity. That includes making every meeting a working one, with engagement rather than speeches and collaboration rather than announcements.

. . . .

If you have the same schedule and time allocation today as you had in 2019, you are pretending that the pandemic never happened.

. . . .

We write with a sense of urgency. As this book goes to press, more than a million of our fellow citizens in the United States, and vastly more around the world, have been lost to the pandemic. Millions more are traumatized as they return to school. Educational systems face a series of stark choices. First, we can ignore it. (Hint—if you have the same schedule and time allocation today as you had in 2019, you are pretending that the pandemic never happened.) Second, we can wish for educational alchemy, in which the right mix of technology and rapid speech will make up for the fact that we have second graders who can't read and middle schoolers who are lost in every sentence of their textbooks. Or we can choose the path of engagement—confident that in order for learning, teaching, and leadership to succeed, relationships through effective engagement must come first. If you choose the third way, you are in the right place.

CHAPTER ONE

Connections

Relationships Are Essential for Engagement

iStock.com/Drazen Zigic

In this chapter, you will learn about . . .

- The essential nature of relationships
- The components of safe and meaningful relationships
- Common mistakes in relationship building
- Student leadership: the superglue of social relationships
- Establishing, restoring, and maintaining staff relationships

In a synthesis of scientific research on the factors that most contributed to healthy living and especially healthy aging, confident and secure relationships topped the list (Evans 2018). If relationships are essential for the health of retirees, who have had a lifetime to learn how to navigate friendships, romantic partners, breakups, and the losses and joys of relationships, then how much more difficult must the development and maintenance of relationships be for students? As older people in successful long-term relationships know, one of the keys is commitment. That is, effective relationships are not transactional—"I'll do this for you if but only if you do this for me." And telling students to "go out and make some friends" is about as helpful as telling their single teachers and administrators to go to a bar and find a mate. Perhaps it's possible, but the evidence suggests that we must take the importance of relationships much more seriously and give children the time and space that they need to learn not only how to establish relationships but also how to deal with the inevitable challenges that relationships with peers and adults entail.

· ·

Telling students to "go out and make some friends" is about as helpful as telling their single teachers and administrators to go to a bar and find a mate.

· ·

We begin this chapter with a summary of the evidence of why relationships are so important. They affect the physical and mental health of our students and colleagues and, when schools leave little time for relationship building because of the exigencies of schedules, testing, and endlessly structured activities, there is little time or opportunity for relationships to flourish. We recognize that because there have been cases of abusive relationships among staff members and between staff and students, the entire idea of an adult-student relationship may be threatening or even scary. Thus, we consider the components of safe and meaningful relationships. Unsafe relationships are manipulative and dangerous. Safe and meaningful relationships are those that demonstrate unconditional support for our students and colleagues in which they know they are accepted and supported even when they make mistakes. We then turn our attention to common mistakes in relationship building. Students know a phony a mile away, and when formulaic relationship-building activities are implemented in schools within an environment that is threatening, humiliating, and shaming, we should not be surprised if students are skeptical to think that a packaged game or exercise will fix that.

. . . .

There is no greater threat than that of the bombardment of dopamine provided by technology when a student sits alone in the dark with a device, devoid of human interaction.

. . . .

Next, we consider common threats to relationships, and in the third decade of the 21st century, there is no greater threat than that of the bombardment of dopamine provided by technology when a student sits alone in the dark with a device, devoid of human interaction. The second-by-second reinforcement of these interactions literally alters the brains of students and leads them to be disinterested in something as boring as a human who fails to provide the likes, emojis, and other forms of reinforcement that their nonhuman technology companions can provide.

Teachers and administrators cannot bear responsibility for relationship building alone. There is a critical role that student leaders must play in this vital element of school life. We're not just talking about team captains and class presidents, but about the web of informal student leaders who can have a powerful impact—for good or ill—on school culture. Finally, we consider how school leaders and teachers can dramatically improve the quality of adult relationships. Even in a time that is overwhelmingly busy, with shortages of teachers, substitutes, and bus drivers, there are specific things that educators can and must do to demonstrate their commitment to safe and effective relationships in every school. At the end of the chapter, we offer specific suggestions about what readers can do now—today—to strengthen relationships in your building.

THE ESSENTIAL NATURE OF RELATIONSHIPS

The positive impact of student-teacher relationships on the long-term academic and social development of students is well established in the scientific literature (Rimm-Kaufma and Sandilos 2010). As a result of the pervasive school closures during the global pandemic, teachers also saw first-hand the impact of the absence of relationships. Although many teachers and school administrators worked exceptionally long hours and schools invested billions of dollars on technology to link students to their schools, the vast majority of students did not establish and maintain the relationships necessary for a positive learning environment (Hari 2022). Even students with superior technology proficiency, such as those studying at the Massachusetts Institute of Technology (MIT), required what their professors called human time—the ability to interact with a three-dimensional human—that even some of the smartest college students on the planet may otherwise lack (Turkle 2016).

Part of the resistance to effective teacher-student relationships is the feeling that the most important adult-student relationship should be with families, not teachers. This is a false dichotomy. Certainly, parents are the first, most enduring, and most important teachers that children will ever have. Nevertheless, as children grow older, the conversations with a trusted teacher can be different in tone and content than the conversations they have with their caregivers. This is especially true of adolescents who may not be willing to have conversations about development, sexuality, and other challenging subjects with parents (Scherr 2020). Few people doubt the power of positive relationships for students and staff. The challenge is how to make these relationships safe, deep, and meaningful.

Jerome*, a ninth-grade student at Washington High School, used to love school. Before COVID-related school closures, he excelled in math and wrote prize-winning essays. The oldest of four kids, Jerome took pride not only in his

---

*The student examples in this book are authentic representations of both individual students and composites of more than one student. All of the names have been changed.

academic success but also as a provider for his siblings. Every month, he helped his mom with the rent as a result of his after-school and weekend job. Before his father died, Jerome promised him that he would be the "man of the house" even though he was only 12 at the time. Despite his academic success in middle school, high school has been rough. Ms. Shay, his English teacher, recognized Jerome's great writing gifts. While he rarely turned in homework, Jerome was diligent and attentive in class and was able to complete responses to literature and persuasive essays quickly during the time Ms. Shay allowed students to work in class.

But algebra was a different story. For Mr. Knox, class periods were dominated by his lectures, and student success depended upon the completion of voluminous homework. Some of the concepts were familiar, as Jerome had mastered pre-algebra in middle school. But other concepts were bewildering, and when Mr. Knox asked, "Anybody got any questions?" it was very clear that the expected response was silence. One day, after failing a quiz, Jerome heard Mr. Knox say, "I can see we've got a bunch of real geniuses here," and Jerome felt that the insult was directed at him. Mr. Knox continued, "I told you that you could come in after school, but none of you did, so if you failed, that's on you." Every day after school, Jerome was working, not playing video games or hanging out with friends, as his teacher imagined. As he heard Mr. Knox's voice, Jerome's temper got the better of him, and he shoved his books off his desk. "To the office!" ordered Mr. Knox. Jerome walked out, not to the office, but off the campus entirely, wondering if he should return.

If Ms. Shay was a positive influence and Mr. Knox was a negative influence, doesn't it all balance out? In *The Power of Bad*, professor Roy Baumeister's research is conclusive—bad memories overwhelm positive ones (Tierny and Baumeister 2019). The power of positive relationships is evident and the source of our greatest memories as teachers. Our best days as teachers and leaders are not only at school, but in the casual encounters years after, when students see us in the street, store, or public gathering and ask, "Do you remember me? You really made a difference in my life." These are the relationship highs, and they are wonderful. But we fail to recognize relationship lows at our peril. A single Mr. Knox can poison a well of Ms. Shays.

The psychological research from Baumeister and colleagues is clear that we not only retain negative memories but perseverate about them. When those negative experiences happen to several students, it causes what Boston College professor Belle Liang calls *co-rumination,* the phenomenon in which a mishap for one student can quickly become a catastrophe for a group of students.

THE COMPONENTS OF SAFE AND MEANINGFUL RELATIONSHIPS

The Search Institute suggests a framework for building and maintaining effective relationships. Although the framework was written with student-teacher relationships in mind, the elements of the framework could be applied to relationships throughout a school and district, whether it is among teachers and administrators, a cabinet, a family group, or a governing board. Some of the key components of the framework are the following, expressed from the point of view of the student or colleague with whom we are trying to build a relationship:

Show me that I matter to you.

Be someone I can trust.

Really pay attention when we are together.

Make me feel known and valued.

Show me you enjoy being with me.

Praise me for my efforts and achievements.

Push me to keep getting better.

Expect me to live up to my potential.

Push me to go further.

Insist that I take responsibility for my actions.

Help me learn from mistakes and setbacks.

Help me complete tasks and achieve goals.

Guide me through hard situations.

Build my confidence and help me to take charge of my life.

Stand up for me when I need it.

Put limits in place that keep me on track.

Share power.

Treat me with respect and give me a say.

Take me seriously and treat me fairly.

Involve me in decisions that affect me.

Work with me to solve problems and reach goals.

Create opportunities for me to take action and lead.

Connect me with people and places that broaden my world.

Inspire me to see possibilities for my future.

Expose me to new ideas, experiences, and places.

Introduce me to people who can help me grow.

Source: Search Institute 2018. The Developmental Relationships Framework is copyrighted by Search Institute, Minneapolis, MN (www.searchinstitute.org) and used with permission.

These ideas are equally applicable to kindergarten teachers helping students navigate their first experiences at school and to the principal helping teachers deal with the complex and sometimes bewildering challenges of our profession. The through-line of all these ideas is respect and decency. It is not the absence of limits and rules, but rather the use of expectations that are not always dependent upon external authority. We have seen too many school leaders extol the values of teacher-student relationships, and then make decisions without involving teachers that struck some of them as arbitrary and capricious. Similarly, we have seen schools in which students are expected to learn from mistakes and bounce back from them, but where classroom observations are mechanistic and evaluative, with little or no input from the classroom teacher who is being observed. In other words, the same consideration about learning from errors is not extended to their teachers.

The fundamental conclusion is that we know that quality relationships with students have a profound and lasting impact on their social and academic success. Moreover, we know how to develop and sustain those relationships. But those efforts will fail if we do not recall that engagement, and the relationships on which engagement depends, must be predicated on a system that places equal importance on trust and respect among adults. Without that, we can't expect that teachers will have the capacity to do the same toward students.

COMMON MISTAKES IN RELATIONSHIP BUILDING

Whenever we hear a school leader giving a speech about the importance of relationships and commitment in schools, we are struck by the irony. If relationships were really that important, wouldn't a conversation be a better format than a speech? It's not unlike what happens in universities when we advocate fiercely for the value of collaborative learning, and then require doctoral students to write a dissertation on that subject entirely alone. The biggest mistake we have observed in relationship building is when the actions of leaders do not match their rhetoric. You don't build relationships with students and colleagues with a tool kit, workshop, or speech. You build relationships by taking the risks required to engage directly with students and colleagues.

. . . .

The biggest mistake we have observed in relationship building is when the actions of leaders do not match their rhetoric.

. . . .

It all starts with the name. We know principals of schools with more than 1,000 students who make it a daily discipline to engage students by name. They are always in the hallways during passing periods and in the bus lane or pickup area at the beginning and end of every day. They leave no doubt that a heavy class load, even when some secondary teachers may have 180 students during the day, is never an excuse for not knowing the name of every student. They also make a point of knowing something about them, and in particular, they build relationships with students who sometimes are more comfortable being anonymous. It's easy to have a relationship with the Superintendent's Advisory Committee, the National Honor Society members, or the captains of championship athletic teams. The challenge of relationship building is more complex for the students who glide through the hallways, avoiding eye contact with peers, teachers, and administrators. They sit in the back of the class, rarely cause trouble, and value those easy days when they are never called upon because they never raise their hands or otherwise call attention to themselves.

This environment leads to another common mistake in building relationships with students. Well-intentioned adults assume that the students just want to be left alone. As we heard one teacher say, "We have an agreement—we don't make them work too hard if they don't make us work too hard." It's a sullen truce, a joyless environment, and few people take the risk of opening a dialogue if it might be uncomfortable. Anyone who has taught or parented adolescents has experienced the monosyllabic replies to the usual litany of questions:

How was school? *Fine.*

Make any friends? *No.*

Anything interesting happen? *No.*

Have any homework? *A little.*

Worried about anything? *No.*

The mistake we make is to accept that this life of solitude, isolated from friends and teachers, is what the students really want. The truth is that students of all ages, and especially adolescents, crave to be known, noticed, and cared for. In one major metropolitan school system, we interviewed students who had dropped out. Said one student, "I just stopped coming—and nobody noticed. Nobody even called my mom for more than three months. They didn't care if I was there or not."

The greatest threat to relationships in any school is the unwavering specter of evaluation, with students valued only for their test performance and teachers only valued for their ability to conform to the latest edition of the checklist that administrators use to evaluate—and evaluate and evaluate. Since the advent of No Child Left Behind in 2001 and its successor legislation, the prevailing theory among state departments of education has been that teachers and students can be evaluated into success. That hypothesis, having been tested for more than two decades, is, to put it mildly, unsupported by the evidence. While we understand the need for policy makers to understand how students are progressing, the use of student evaluation as a club rather than a diagnostic tool has led to a climate of fear that pervades nearly every school in the spring of each year. Similarly, teacher evaluation systems have consumed hundreds of millions of dollars and untold hours of time, with no evidence to suggest that any teacher was ever evaluated into more effective professional practices. This situation has created an atmosphere that is the opposite of effective relationships, with students fearing teachers, teachers fearing administrators, and conversations about teaching and learning that might have been constructive instead becoming adversarial, combative, and unproductive. There are far better alternatives to make teacher observation and student data analysis more effective, replacing evaluation with coaching (Marshall and Marshal 2017). A globally recognized leader in teacher observation, Kim Marshall makes the powerful case that the extremes of evaluation as a threat or, just as bad, the complete absence of meaningful classroom observations, fails to advance the cause of improved teaching and learning. Rather, frequent observations, with very specific feedback, along with the opportunity for the teachers to use the feedback to improve, lead to collaboration and a spirit of collective improvement—precisely what is needed to maintain strong relationships. In *The Progress Principle*, Harvard Business School professors make the compelling case that we are far more engaged and motivated with indications of very frequent—even daily—progress, than by the yawning gap that typically separates performance from feedback (Amabile and Kramer 2011). We are seeing teachers jettison 40-item unit tests, often administered weeks after the relevant lessons were presented, with daily mini-assessments of two or three items, daily checks for understanding, with immediate feedback to students. These techniques transform feedback from an accusation into an opportunity for dialogue, learning, and, most importantly, progress.

. . . .

The use of student evaluation as a club rather than a diagnostic tool has led to a climate of fear that pervades nearly every school in the spring of each year.

. . . .

The final common mistake in building and maintaining relationships is that we give up when the going is tough. Any reader who has been in a serious adult relationship for more than about two weeks understands that relationships are hard, and ecstasy can turn to acrimony in a moment and sometimes over something trivial. Similarly, the star student who is diligent and compliant can, in the space of a weekend, turn glum, defiant, and disengaged. The colleague who always volunteers in a staff meeting to share ideas can become silent and seething with anger, the source of which is a mystery. Our impulse in these cases may be to just give students and staff the space and isolation that they appear to want. Perhaps that is appropriate, but if we do not inquire, if we don't take the time to learn the source of these changes, then we are inserting our own presumptions in the place of facts known only to those students and colleagues. Saying to the suddenly silent person, "Hi—I wondered if we could talk for a minute," might lead to an essential conversation or it might lead to them storming off in a rage. In education, it's worthwhile reminding ourselves that if it were easy, somebody else would be doing it.

STUDENT LEADERSHIP: THE SUPERGLUE OF SOCIAL RELATIONSHIPS

While we believe that the greatest degree of responsibility for relationship building rests with teachers and school leaders, we also know that excluding students from shared responsibility for relationship building is an inherent contradiction. The students are not empty vessels into which we pour our empathy, wisdom, and relationship skills. When students take the lead—not just in typical sports or clubs, but in a variety of activities, ranging from newly invented groups devoted to activism, cooking, exploration, technology, and as many ideas as the minds of students can create—then the admonitions of adults are replaced with the voices of peers. "You missed the meeting yesterday—we need you here!" is more powerful coming from a peer than the orations on the value of attendance and diligence that adults might provide.

. . . .

When students went from zero activities to just two during the year, their grade-point averages jumped by almost two full points, from D to B level grades.

. . . .

The evidence on the power of student leadership is striking. It is not surprising that students who are involved in extracurricular activities have better academic performance, attendance, and behavior than students who are not engaged in any of these activities. What is surprising is the greatest impact of student engagement in extracurricular activities is not with the three-letter athlete or two-club president, but with the completely disengaged student. That is, when students went from zero activities to just two during the year, their grade-point averages jumped by almost two full points, from D to B level grades. But when students increased participation from four activities to five, six, seven, or more, the impact was negligible (Reeves 2021c). We have also seen schools making a decisive commitment to broaden student leadership opportunities beyond the most popular or vocal students. One fifth-grade classroom has a new class president every week. Other schools, in reaction to student resistance to joining clubs or activities, moved club meetings to the middle of the school day, during and adjacent to lunch periods, so no one was excluded for lack of after-school transportation or the requirements of sibling care or jobs. Finally, we cannot avoid noticing that there are schools where 100% participation in extracurricular activities and student leadership opportunities is commonplace. In small rural schools, every single student is needed not just for the athletics teams, but for service clubs, music, and drama—every single student has a role to play outside of the classroom. The other place where we find 100% student engagement in extracurricular activities is in elite independent schools, where parents routinely pay tuition in excess of $50,000 per year. We don't begrudge these parents their economic success, but we do wonder, why is it that rich kids routinely receive leadership and extracurricular activities that are available to only a fraction of similarly capable students in the vast majority of public schools? If engagement and relationships are important for the children of wealthy families, do students in other schools deserve any less?

ESTABLISHING, RESTORING, AND MAINTAINING STAFF RELATIONSHIPS

Teacher and administrator turnover was increasing at an alarming rate before the global pandemic (Phillips 2015; Reeves 2018). After two years of the physical and mental toll associated not only with COVID, but also with community protests for and against masks, for and against school re-openings, and for and against a range of books and curricula, many teachers have had enough. The turnover rate of teachers, which was 8% in 2018, has risen to over 20% in many areas. According to the U.S. Bureau of Labor Statistics, around 600,000 teachers in public education quit between January 2020 and March 2022. In New Mexico, half the superintendents are in their first year, and our observation of the national trend is that senior leaders and board members are unwilling to continue to accept the public abuse and threats to themselves and their families that are all too common. In this climate in which bullying, abuse, and threats are normalized, how can leaders establish relationships among the staff that are positive and encouraging?

. . . .

Teacher and administrator turnover was increasing at an alarming rate before the global pandemic.

. . . .

The advice earlier in this chapter about building positive and respectful relationships with students applies equally well to every teacher and administrator. Teachers need to know, for example, that administrators will have their back when a student reports to a parent or, incredibly in some states, to an anonymous tip line, that the teacher is expressing an idea that is not on the required script. We must not only tolerate divergent thinking but expect it—even assign it—so that students and staff members are comfortable with civil discourse. In staff meetings, debates about choices in curricula, schedules, and other activities should be vigorous and respectful. When the decision is made, it will always be a better informed and wiser decision as the result of discussion rather than silent assent (Beshears and Gino 2015).

One important way that leaders can build relationships with staff members is to radically reconstruct the way that meetings are conducted. When we interviewed a principal who was able to have common formative assessments, collaborative scoring, and a host of other professional learning activities that other principals in the same district claimed were impossible, she explained simply, "I haven't had a staff meeting for three years." She did have meetings—they were part of the schedule and bargaining agreement. But she never read aloud announcements to staff members and never allowed meetings to be diverted into grandstanding. Every meeting was purposeful and screamed respect for teachers and the time that they needed to be effective. Whenever we hear leaders claim that "they don't have the time" for an essential practice, we know it to be a factually untrue statement because every school on the planet has the same number of hours in the day, and every school within a district has an almost identical schedule. The difference is not the time available, but the leadership choices—or the leader's default to historical choices made many years before—about how to use that time. Similarly, cabinet meetings (usually the senior leaders in the district)—often the single most expensive meeting in a district—can be radically transformed with a commitment to use those meetings for deliberation and inquiry rather than presentations (Reeves 2020b).

We know some schools that devote time monthly to wellness checks—checking in on the staff and their families. Sometimes these are private conversations and other times shared with a group, but no meaningful professional learning will take place when staff members feel that their leadership is indifferent to the health of teachers and families. We know of school leaders who have a daily ritual of one-to-one appreciation of staff members. These are not trophies presented in ceremonies, but individual and meaningful acts of appreciation—perhaps a word, a short note—the sort of thing that will linger long after the general and unspecific "thank you" to a group would have evaporated.

. . . .

Leaders will be forgiven for many mistakes, but if they lack credibility and trust, their expertise in every other leadership domain is without value.

. . . .

While most of our discussion of staff relationships has focused on school-level relationships among teachers and school administrators, there is also important evidence on how relationships between district offices and schools can support, or undermine, school performance. While it is hardly news that trust, innovation, and efficacy are vitally important for student and school performance, a study found that the forces that undermined these three key attributes were most likely at the central office level rather than the schools (Daly et al. 2015). Even when efficacy—often cited as one of the most important variables influencing student achievement—was strong, a lack of trust at the highest levels of the organization undermined the impact of efficacy on student achievement. This is consistent with the large-scale study on credibility that concluded that leaders will be forgiven for many mistakes, but if they lack credibility and trust, their expertise in every other leadership domain is without value (Kouzes 2011). The relationship-damaging mistrust that leaders engender is not necessarily deliberate. But the casual statements such as "We value innovation and it's okay to make mistakes!" are undermined when mistakes in pursuit of innovation lead to punishment or humiliation. Skillful teachers know that they must adapt to the daily conditions of the classroom and their students, but if they fear that deviations from the script will lead to sanctions, then don't expect those skillful adaptations, turning on a dime to meet the needs of a student or seizing a creative opportunity to drive home a lesson, to occur.

WHAT TEACHERS AND LEADERS CAN DO NOW

In order to optimize connections—the first key to engagement—consider these ideas that you can implement immediately:

1. Create "human time" in every classroom. This means no devices, even if brought from home, no earphones, and no other diversions. Everyone, including the teacher, attends personally to the discussion at hand, in pairs, small groups, and whole class. Try it for just 45 minutes. If they can do this at MIT, you can do it in your school.

2. Establish the expectation that every staff member, from the newest teacher to the most veteran principal, knows the name of every student and knows something about that student aside from their class performance and most recent test score.

3. Ask three students, "How do you know that your teachers and administrators care about you as a person?" Then just listen. Don't suggest answers. Just listen.

4. Transform staff meetings into a time to get real work done. Never make verbal announcements to college-educated adults who can read them or get them in a Vimeo or voice mail. Change the format and purpose of cabinet meetings to require effective inquiry and decision making and not be a captive audience for senior leaders.

5. Get a list of students in your school who are involved in nothing—no clubs, sports, or other activities—and create a plan to invite them to engage in at least one activity this week. If you need to establish some new clubs and games, then do so.

CHAPTER TWO

Conditions

High Expectations, Attendance, and Participation Are Necessary for Engagement

iStock.com/SeventyFour

In this chapter, you will learn about . . .

- Condition I: Communicate high expectations
- Condition 2: An investment in attendance
- Condition 3: Active participation in learning

There are several conditions that are important if students are to engage in meaningful learning experiences. At the most obvious level, if students are not attending classes, it's hard for them to engage. Assuming there are meaningful experiences to be had in the classroom, missing class stalls learning. Of course, just showing up is not enough. Students also need to participate in the various tasks designed by their teachers. There are a number of effective participation techniques that invite students into thinking and learning, as well as techniques that ensure students interact with their peers in meaningful ways. The tasks and experiences that are assigned to students convey the expectations that educators have. The question is whether these experiences are challenging and convey the belief that students can perform at high levels.

Importantly, what we expect of ourselves at the organizational level influences what we expect of our students. The limits that we place on ourselves constrain what we expect from learners (Mehta and Fine 2019). In this chapter, we use the lens of high expectations to address issues of attendance and participation in engagement.

CONDITION 1: COMMUNICATE HIGH EXPECTATIONS

Much has been written on the influence of expectations on student learning. At the individual level, the expectations a teacher has for a student impact their performance, for better or worse. Hattie's mega-meta-analysis of teacher expectations, comprising 613 studies, yields an effect size of 0.42, meaning that it holds the potential to accelerate student learning (visiblelearningmetax.com). An effect size is a statistical tool that demonstrates the power of a given influence. When several individual studies are aggregated, the effect size across the studies allows for generalizations that explain the overall impact.

However, supporting research demonstrates that a teacher's expectations of students can be influenced by biases and by past performance (see Murdock-Perriera and Sedlacek 2018 for a review). What can emerge is a complex stew where the characteristics of the student become the explanation for why they fail to progress. In doing so, teachers dismiss their influence on students' learning. In dismissing their influence, they turn away from the truth about their own power—that "achievement for *all* is changeable (and not fixed)" (Hattie 2009:35). When attribution for success is focused on student demographics to the exclusion of what a skilled teacher can accomplish, subconscious beliefs about progress take hold. It becomes the luck of the draw. The relative progress of students is viewed as fate rather than opportunity. This undermines the oft-expressed sentiment that "I believe all children can learn."

. . . .

Research demonstrates that a teacher's expectations of students can be influenced by biases and by past performance (see Murdock-Perriera and Sedlacek 2018 for a review).

. . . .

High-Expectation Teaching

Do our practices match our words? Researcher Christine Rubie-Davies has dedicated her work to understanding how teacher expectations influence the achievement of students. It comes as no surprise that students whose teachers have lower expectations of them learn less than peers in high-expectation classrooms. Our behaviors telegraph our beliefs. She found that low-expectation teachers

- Use ability grouping for activities
- Rarely provide students with choice
- Ask more closed rather than open-ended questions
- Praise or criticize based on accuracy
- Ask other students for the correct answer when a student is wrong
- Manage behavior reactively

The good news is that high-expectation practices can be taught. Students in one study whose teachers were trained in high-expectation practices increased their math scores equivalent to three months' worth of gains compared to peers in other classrooms (Rubie-Davies et al. 2015). The secret? Professional learning linked to self-assessment. Teachers watched videos of themselves and scored their own observed practices against what they had learned. The result was that they made changes to their classroom practices that, in turn, elevated their expectations.

High-Expectation Practices in the Classroom

The ways we organize our classrooms for instruction, partner with students in their learning, and use language to uplift have the cumulative effect of communicating what we expect of our students. These three dimensions of practice distinguish the differences between high- and low-expectation teachers.

- **Nondifferentiation of learning.** High-expectation teachers avoid ability grouping students within the classroom during learning tasks. True to the work of Tomlinson (2014), but too often misinterpreted, is the central principle that all learners engage in complex and challenging tasks. In low-expectation classrooms, the misapplication of differentiation is used as an excuse for assigning low-level, repetitive assignments to some students as a tool for remediation. High-expectation teachers adopt an acceleration mindset for all learners and create a range of experiences that students can choose from. The result of using choice is that students are more likely to complete tasks they have selected.

. . . .

High-expectation teachers avoid ability grouping students within the classroom during learning tasks.

. . . .

- **Warm classroom environment.** The second feature of high-expectation classrooms is the emotional climate of the classroom. This comes from an emphasis on knowing each child well and developing a positive relationship with them. Because these teachers use a proactive approach to potential problematic behaviors, they spend less time reprimanding, repeating directions, and reteaching procedures. Perhaps most importantly, they ensure that all students have opportunities to learn. High-expectation teachers are emotionally responsive and use respectful and caring language with all their students.

- **Goal setting and feedback.** The third dimension of high-expectation practices is aligned with setting goals with students, monitoring progress with them, and promoting autonomy and decision making. Many of these practices center on the use of formative evaluation as a tool for students to gauge their own progress. In doing so, high-expectation teachers create a space for young people to view their own learning, rather than being wholly dependent on the teacher to tell them when they've learned something. The net effect is that students become intrinsically motivated. Their sense of agency (which is to say, their belief that they can achieve their goals) increases.

CONDITION 2: AN INVESTMENT IN ATTENDANCE

At the risk of stating the obvious, engagement can't happen if a student isn't there. Even as schools have reopened, districts around the country report unprecedented levels of absentee-ism. The reasons are varied, but the picture is complicated by COVID-19 mitigation techniques including quarantining, as well as surges such as those witnessed in January 2022 when many districts reported that daily attendance dipped below 70%. One immediate result was that teachers were faced with an even more challenging landscape as they tried to predict who might be in attendance on a given day and who had missed instruction.

However, these more recent developments magnify an already troubling attendance picture. According to the Civil Rights Data Collection (2019), during the 2015–2016 school year, more than 7 million students representing 16% of the popu-lation were chronically absent, defined as missing 15 or more days in a single school year. This varies by grade level and peaks in high school, with 20% of students chronically absent. And this is not uniformly distributed. Students of color, Indigenous students, and students with disabilities are more likely to be chronically absent. Those numbers represent 100 million days of instruction lost. That's 100 million unrealized opportunities to engage learners.

Responses to Chronic Absenteeism

Conventional responses to absenteeism have been confined mostly to the individual students and their families and are primarily punitive in nature. Truancy boards are particularly prevalent in districts that report high levels of chronic absenteeism. However, these and other interventions seem to have relatively little impact. A meta-analysis of 22 studies on attendance interventions grouped them into three categories: behavioral interventions, family-school partnerships, and academic interventions (Eklund et al. 2020). They reported that most studies (64%) were behaviorally oriented, with the rest comprised of interventions that involved a family member or teaching the student-specific academic skills. Regardless of the approach, all had only a small positive effect on changing the attendance trajectory of students.

. . . .

Chronic absenteeism is a sign that positive conditions for learning are missing (Chang et al. 2019).

. . . .

Perhaps something is being overlooked. Chronic absenteeism is a sign that positive conditions for learning are missing (Chang et al. 2019). Rather than relying solely on the individual student as the unit of analysis, we are challenged to view chronic absenteeism through the lens of engagement and high expectations. We invite you to reconsider the markers of high-expectation teachers through the lens of our institutions:

- Nondifferentiation of high expectations for all students

- Warm school environment

- Bidirectional goal setting and feedback to improve school conditions while strengthening students and families

Students vote with their feet. A business that lacks foot traffic must either adapt or disappear. Blaming the customer without examining the business model is a recipe for failure. The extent to which students fail to engage with schooling is feedback to us about the conditions of schooling. We need to add to our toolkit by expanding our view to look closely at individual student factors while also having the courage to examine how we might improve the conditions needed to bring them back.

. . . .

The extent to which students fail to engage with schooling is feedback to us about the conditions of schooling.

. . . .

A Coordinated System of Supports for Attendance

There has been promising work on re-engaging students who are chronically absent at a systems level. The Early Warning Intervention (EWI) team model consists of a multidisciplinary team of academic and nonacademic personnel (Davis et al. 2019). This system was developed by researchers at Johns Hopkins University and the National High School Center to provide a more coherent means of assisting students who are showing a higher risk of academic failure (Marken et al. 2020). It has since been implemented for middle grades as well and is now being used in 31 states. The indicators fall across three broad categories, called the *ABCs*: attendance, behavior, and course completion (Davis et al. 2019). Each of these is predictive of falling behind and dropping out; the risk increases exponentially when multiple indicators are present:

- **Attendance.** The student is absent (excused or unexcused) for 20% of instructional time.

- **Behavior.** According to locally validated measures, the student has been suspended (in-school or out-of-school) or has received multiple behavioral referrals.

- **Course completion.** The student has failed a mathematics or English course.

The team is led by an adult in the school who serves as a facilitator for team meetings and is a central figure for coordinated communication. In addition, there is a member of the team who can serve as a liaison between home and school. This person might be a full-time parent education coordinator, or the role might be spread among several school members assigned by grade level.

Unlike other models, re-engagement is not the sole responsibility of those one or two people. Rather, every adult in the school is a potential member, depending on the student. These teams meet biweekly to discuss interventions, progress, and barriers across three markers (Davis et al. 2019). Importantly, these provide schools with feedback to them about the levers of schooling, namely high expectations for all, and a warm school climate, using a continuous cycle of improvement fueled by feedback and goal setting for the organization.

CONDITION 3: ACTIVE PARTICIPATION IN LEARNING

Getting students to school is an important condition that must be present for engagement in learning. Once they are in a learning environment, whether in-person, online, or blended, students need to participate in learning tasks. Of course, those tasks need to be worth their effort, and students who find relevance in their learning are much more likely to participate. We are not suggesting that participation equals engagement, but rather that participating in learning tasks is a condition that can foster engagement. As Chickering and Ehrmann (1996) noted, "learning is not a spectator sport."

Universal Response

As an example, universal response opportunities provide all students a chance to participate at the same time. This reduces the fear that some students have that their answers will be judged and that they are wrong. Later in this book, we will focus on creating an environment in which struggle is expected and honored, but too many students come to school afraid to participate because they do not want to be wrong, or they are accustomed to others in the class taking charge and sharing answers first.

. . . .

"Learning is not a spectator sport."

. . . .

Universal responses are those techniques used by the teacher to allow for simultaneous replies from every member of the group, rather than isolated answers. A goal of universal response is to solicit answers from all the students to check for understanding and obtain a sense of whether the instruction is sticking or not.

The benefits of universal response opportunities are twofold:

- They provide you a chance to get a quick read on student understanding in real time.

- These micro-assessments prompt learners to consider their own knowledge in the moment.

The cognitive dissonance that comes from finding out that the reply was incorrect can open a dialogue as they ask questions and seek clarification. In other words, it shifts learning from a passive to an active endeavor. A meta-analysis of 18 studies on the use of preprinted and write-on response cards showed that they were associated with higher achievement on tests and quizzes, higher levels of participation, and lower levels of disruptive behavior, compared to individual hand raising to answer a question (Randolph 2007).

Examples of universal response abound in face-to-face classrooms. Teachers routinely use response cards and student whiteboards to gain a sense of what each child can do. Another example is when students use hand signals, such as a fist-to-five signaling their agreement about a state-ment, or a thumbs up–thumbs down response for dichot-omous questions, such as yes/no or true/false. We can also use polls and chat features of online programs for universal response.

The key is to invite students to participate in universal response opportunities at least every 10 minutes (and maybe more frequently). In doing so, you can start to build a memory trace because of the multiple opportunities students have to retrieve information from their brains. Parenthetically, this allows you to adjust the lesson based on the responses you receive from students, which can keep the students focused on new learning rather than things that they already know. In doing so, students are much more likely to be engaged.

. . . .

Invite students to participate in universal response opportunities at least every 10 minutes (and maybe more frequently).

. . . .

Cole (2017) organized active participation techniques into three categories (for a list of their techniques, see the appendix):

1. Active participation through oral responses

2. Active participation through written responses

3. Active participation through action responses

There are so many techniques that educators can use to invite students to participate. The point is that we need to use them. In fact, we probably need to redouble our efforts to invite students to participate, especially through universal response tools.

Increasing Student-to-Student Interaction

We imagine by now that you are wondering when we are going to utter the word most associated with engagement: *motivation*. How often have you heard a student described as "unmotivated"? Further, their "lack of motivation" is the reason why they aren't engaged. To us, it is a version of the statement, "I taught them. They just didn't learn it." In the motivation version, it's "I teach lessons. They just aren't motivated."

We must be intentional in our efforts to create opportunities to foster motivation. This isn't about the extrinsic rewards of points, grades, and "Fun Friday" but rather ensuring that there are lots of opportunities for student-to-student interaction. In fact, meaningful learning interactions with peers are associated with motivation and school satisfaction. As one example, a study of fourth through sixth graders found that students of color in math classrooms that used cooperative and collaborative learning reported significantly more positive attitudes about the subject (Vaughan 2002).

Develop Routines That Convey High Expectations

We'll return to Rubie-Davies' (2014) work on high-expectation teaching, this time through the lens of student-to-student interactions. Among her findings in this realm are to

- Use mixed-ability groupings and change groupings frequently

- Encourage students to work with a range of their peers

- Give students responsibility for their learning

- Allow all learners to engage in advanced activities

- Establish routines and procedures at the beginning of the school year

This last indicator bridges theory to practice. Identify routines that promote meaningful interaction for all students. In doing so, learners experience more frequent touchpoints of active engagement with peers rather than passive reception of information. These routines, once taught, provide the additional benefit of recouping time that is otherwise consumed by giving instructions while sacrificing peer interactions. Don't fall for the canard that you need to "change it up" all the time to "keep it fresh." Identify a handful of high-utility collaborative routines that you can utilize frequently. While by no means an exhaustive list, we have developed a range of student-to-student interactions that promote elements of high expectations and increase active participation.

· ·

Don't fall for the canard that you need to "change it up" all the time to "keep it fresh." Identify a handful of high-utility collaborative routines that you can utilize frequently.

· ·

- **Busy bees.** This routine is useful in primary classrooms. Students mimic the buzzing sound and slow movement of bumblebees as they buzz around the room to find a partner. When the teacher says, "Busy bees, fly!" students move around the room and buzz until they hear, "Busy bees, land!" The "bee" they are standing next to becomes their partner for a brief learning activity such as giving an opinion, answering a question, or solving a math problem.

- **Inside/outside circles.** Two concentric circles of students stand or sit to face one another. The teacher poses a question to the class, and the partners respond briefly to one another. At the signal, the outer circle rotates one position to the left to face a new partner. The conversation continues for several rounds. For each rotation, students may respond to the same prompt or to a different but related one.

- **Collaborative posters.** In groups, students create a poster representing the main ideas of the concept. Students are given a rubric that describes what must be included in the poster. After thinking individually about how to represent their ideas, each student selects one color of pen and uses only that color on the chart. All students must contribute to both writing and drawing on the poster and sign it. Posters are displayed in the room so that students evaluate their own poster and at least one other using the rubric.

- **Explorers and settlers.** Assign half the students to be explorers and the other half to be settlers. Explorers seek out a settler to discuss a question. Repeat the process one to two times to discuss the same question or a new, related question.

- **Four corners.** Assign each corner of the room a category related to the topic. Tell the students the four categories and ask them to write down which category they are most interested in, along with two to three reasons for their choice. They then form groups by going to the corner of the room labeled with the category they selected. In groups of three to four students, they share their reasons for their selection. This is also another way to form groups to complete an assigned task.

- **Reciprocal teaching.** Students work in groups of four with a common piece of text. Each member has a role: summarizer, questioner, clarifier, and predictor (Palincsar and Brown 1986). These roles closely mirror the kinds of reading comprehension strategies necessary for understanding expository text. The reading is chunked into shorter passages so that the group can stop to discuss periodically.

- **Jigsaw.** Each student in the class has two memberships: a home group and an expert group. Each home group of four members meets to discuss the task and divide the work according to the teacher's directions. After each home group member has their task, they move to expert groups comprised of members with the same task. The expert groups meet to read and discuss their portion of the assignment and practice how they will teach it when they return to their home groups. Students teach their expert portion to home group members and learn about the other sections of the reading. Finally, they return once more to their expert groups to discuss how their topic fits into the larger subject (Aronson 2002).

- **Discussion roundtable.** Students fold a piece of paper into quadrants and record their thinking in the upper left quadrant. This could be from a reading or video. They then take notes in other quadrants as students share their thinking. The final product is then a record of the viewpoints of each member of the group.

- **Text rendering.** Students read a piece of text, focusing on key points. When their group members have finished, each student shares a significant sentence. In the second round, each student shares a significant phrase, which does not need to be within the sentence they chose (and they record these). During the third round, each student shares a word from the reading that resonated with them (and they record these). The group then discusses the ideas generated.

- **Five-word summary.** Students read a piece of text and choose five words that summarize the reading. They then talk with a partner to reach consensus on five words that summarize the reading before joining another partnership. Now the four students reach agreements on the five words that represent the text. From there, they create their own summary of the text, using the five words agreed upon by the group.

Again, these are examples of routines that promote student-to-student interaction and capitalize on motivation and engagement for students. There are many others. But identifying and teaching routines for these interactions makes it more likely that they will be utilized regularly.

WHAT TEACHERS AND LEADERS CAN DO NOW

Commit to creating the conditions necessary for promoting engagement through high-expectation actions.

1. Inventory your high-expectation practices by recording and viewing a 20-minute segment of your instruction. Look for indicators profiled in this chapter, including grouping arrangements, opportunities for interactions, a warm classroom climate, and goal setting and feedback.

2. Do the same at the school level. Revisit your annual school climate survey and examine it through high expectations. How are students grouped across the school? What do families say about how inviting the school feels to them?

3. Examine your attendance data and identify who your chronically absent students are. What does your attendance data look like? Do you have comprehensive supports for chronically absent students?

4. Meet as departments or grade levels to discuss participation practices and routines. Discuss the role of universal response opportunities in the context of your students. Identify and commit to some high-utility student interaction routines and teach them. Schedule follow-up meetings with colleagues to discuss your observations as they relate to engagement.

CHAPTER THREE

Challenge
Dealing With Struggle and Failure

iStock.com/SolStock

In this chapter, you will learn about . . .

- The failure of failure rhetoric
- Getting motivation right
- How shame destroys motivation
- Putting the "L" back in SEL
- Barriers to engagement during challenges
- How leaders model perseverance through challenge
- The psychological safety imperative

We have all heard the rhetoric surrounding failure in schools. "It's just part of learning," the pundits say. "FAIL is First Attempt In Learning," they say. They exhort us to believe that failure is essential for innovation and progress. While all these claims are undoubtedly true, there is a vast difference between the rhetoric of failure and the reality in which students and adults quickly find that failure is not rewarded as a step toward progress, but as a source of shame and embarrassment. In this chapter, we explore the essential nature of challenges in schools and how leaders, teachers, and students can genuinely face the reality of challenges and the failures that accompany them and then, with persistence and perseverance, learn from those failures and succeed. Their success is not merely solving a difficult math problem or staying with a challenging text in literature or science. Rather, the success associated with facing challenges and persevering through them provides lifelong lessons that, research suggests, benefit the students long after their school years (Dweck 2007). The chapter concludes with a discussion of how leaders at every level must model how challenges are faced and overcome.

THE FAILURE OF FAILURE RHETORIC

Contrast the rhetoric of the value of failure with the reality of the reaction to failure by authority figures when mistakes are made by students, teachers, and leaders. Right answers in the classroom are greeted with praise and applause, while wrong answers or silence in response to a question receive a look of disapproval and disappointment. Students believe what we do far more than our words about the value of failure. The expectation that superintendents and other senior leaders provide flawless decisions is the very antithesis of encouraging productive challenges, resilience in the face of error, and the persistence required for effective leadership and learning (Lenz 2015). Students and teachers cannot engage in the deeply complex and personally rewarding task of innovative projects without repeated failures, analysis, learning, and, most importantly, resilience and repeated efforts to succeed. Yet in the same classroom, there is a cloud of forces that militate against failure. In the classroom, students are told that in the real world, they must "get it right the first time." Even on classroom activities that require creativity—the very essence of the need for trial and error—we found that the vast majority of scoring guides that teachers used to evaluate student work on these projects emphasized working independently to get the first attempt performed with perfection (Reeves and Reeves 2016).

· ·

There is a vast difference between the rhetoric of failure and the reality in which students and adults quickly find that failure is not rewarded as a step toward progress.

· ·

The fear of failure is true to an even greater extent in meetings of teachers and leaders where skepticism and questioning can be met with exasperation that the skeptic just doesn't seem to get it and clearly is not a team player. A case in point is the prevailing emphasis on "fidelity" in the implementation of new curriculum materials. We observed a case in which a new math curriculum was accompanied by observational "audits" in which district officials rated, on a zero-to-two scale, the extent to which teachers implemented the curriculum as directed. Equipped with all these ratings, along with the results of interim assessments, it seemed a reasonable question to ask whether higher levels of fidelity, as reflected in the observational ratings, were associated with higher levels of student performance. The question had not occurred to the district officials conducting the observations; they merely assumed that fidelity of implementation of the curriculum alone was a sufficient result. Nevertheless, a quick analysis of the data revealed that the teachers with the highest scores on fidelity did not have greater gains in achievement and, in fact, some had lower gains than their peers with lower fidelity scores. This does not necessarily imply that the curriculum itself was bad, but rather that analyses of fidelity of implementation can measure the wrong thing. While we are not arguing that teachers should be indifferent to the curriculum and lessons associated with it, we also know that skillful teachers must have opportunities to depart from the script to meet the needs of students. For example, these teachers must be able to engage in informal pre-assessment to determine the degree to which students are ready for the lesson at hand. Moreover, the skillful teacher must be able to make on-the-spot decisions to recognize thinking errors by students, stop, re-teach, and re-assess, in order to ensure the greatest levels of student learning. These interruptions are rarely on the script and regarded as part of fidelity of implementation, but skillful teachers nevertheless understand that this is an essential part of their professional responsibilities.

. . . .

Skillful teachers must have opportunities to depart from the script to meet the needs of students.

. . . .

The failure of failure rhetoric is most vividly apparent in senior leadership forums, such as meetings of the cabinet and governing board. These leaders and policy makers tend to be risk averse, and thus the toleration of error—or even the discussion of failure—is easily suppressed.

The rhetoric of failure is closer to the children's book *The Little Engine That Could* ("I think I can, I think I can") than to reality. While the perseverance suggested by the Little Engine is admirable—certainly better than the ethic of getting it right the first time—the reality of the perseverance necessary for breakthrough success is closer to that represented by James Dyson (2021), whose legendary career of innovation began with more than 5,000 failures.

The acid test of whether the rhetoric of the value of failure is consistent with the reality of the classroom and the meetings of teachers and leaders is this question: What happened the last time someone failed? In the case of students, the most common disconnection between rhetoric and the reality of failure is the institutionalized use of the average, in which students are regularly punished at the end of the semester for the mistakes that they made months earlier. The explicit message is, "We don't care how resilient you are or how much you persevere and improve, because we will always hold past failures against you." Teacher evaluations sometimes have the same inherent flaw, with observations throughout the year being averaged to determine a teacher evaluation or, even worse, the evaluation for an entire year coming down to only one or two observations that are part of an elaborate kabuki-like drama in which every move is contrived, and the focus is on the performance rather than on student learning. At the senior leadership and policy maker levels, we must insist that every decision is made with a clear-eyed acknowledgment of the potential advantages and disadvantages of each decision alternative. When, inevitably, some of those potential disadvantages turn out to be part of the reality of the decision maker's lives, then the reason cannot be dismay or recrimination, but a rational reaction that these disadvantages were considered and foreseen, and that leaders have a clearly established plan to react to them.

. . . .

The most common disconnection between rhetoric and the reality of failure is the institutionalized use of the average, in which students are regularly punished at the end of the semester for the mistakes that they made months earlier.

. . . .

If we are to take seriously the abundant science of learning in which failure is an essential part of learning (Argarwal and Bain 2019), then we must systematically value mistakes and learn from them.

GETTING MOTIVATION RIGHT

Ms. Barb, as the students called her, loved candy. Every day one might hear the cash register ring in the office of the local dentist; in her fourth-grade classroom, Ms. Barb handed out candy and jawbreakers for every accomplishment. When students would sit down, raise their hands, cooperate with a partner, read a sentence, or volunteer to clean up the classroom, effusive praise and candy were sure to follow. Ms. Barb knew the research on motivation and sincerely believed that, ultimately, someday, students needed intrinsic motivation to learn. But first, she reasoned, they needed immediate rewards to be motivated to perform. At first, this motivation strategy worked. But ultimately, the students demanded more and more rewards for fewer accomplishments. Being on time morphed into "I was only three minutes late—can't I have a candy?" Hastily scribbled sentences were submitted in a hurry in the hopes of an immediate reward. As with research subjects whose only reward was a sugar high, students were engaged only on the most superficial level and quickly became disengaged if the familiar rewards were not provided (Wood 2019). When the same students went to Ms. Gunz's class in the fifth grade, they were surprised at the absence of candy rewards. Nevertheless, they performed well when, after a few weeks, the genuine reward of competence was provided. They were no longer submitting poor work for a piece of candy, but great work for the reward of knowing that they were really good at something.

One of the most common questions we receive from teachers, parents, and school leaders is, "How do you motivate the unmotivated student?" This is particularly true for adolescent students for whom school and the particular assignment at hand are far from their top priority. Let us begin this discussion on motivation with what a century of research demonstrates does not motivate students: grading (Guskey 2020). Teachers persist in awarding Fs and zeros for missing work and deducting points for late work, apparently believing that because the teachers, when they were students, were motivated by the fear of lost points, that same motivational apparatus would apply to students of today. If this belief were true, however, then decades and centuries of the use of grading as punishment should yield students of today who are motivated to turn in work that is perfect and on time. We know of no teacher on the planet who can say that this reflects current student performance.

. . . .

Let us begin our discussion with what a century of research demonstrates does not motivate students: grading (Guskey 2020).

. . . .

If grades are not the primary motivator of students, then what is? There are four primary motivators that lead to better student engagement and, as a result, higher levels of performance:

- Competence

- Personal significance

- Feedback and progress

- Choice

The sequence of these motivators is significant, as the common presumption is that choice alone is a sufficient motivator for students. While choice is important, it is insufficient as a motivator. This explains the widespread failure of the "cafeteria curriculum" in which students have many choices, including the choice to fail. Indeed, in *The Paradox of Choice,* Swarthmore psychologist Barry Schwartz described experimental research in which too many choices led people not to be satisfied with their smorgasbord of choices, but rather to become paralyzed and make no decision at all (Schwartz 2016).

• •

The most important motivator of all for students—and adults as well—is competence.

• •

The most important motivator of all for students—and adults as well—is competence. Even at relatively low levels of interest, such as the most mindless of video games, students will remain engaged because competence at something—even just shooting space aliens or hitting a ball back and forth—brings a certain dopamine hit to the brain. This is why even the illusion of competence—such as winning at a casino slot machine, accompanied by bells, sirens, and a cash payout (that is consistently lower than the total amount of cash placed into those machines) allows people to feel, at least temporarily, successful and motivated to continue to play the game. A far better standard for competence, however, is being competent at something that matters—that arouses the student's interest and that is personally relevant to them (Gieras 2020). Students quickly label themselves for good or ill: "I'm a really good soccer player" or "I'm just no good at math." A single error—especially one that is public and embarrassing—can lead to a label that persists for a lifetime. How many supremely intelligent and competent adults do you know who describe themselves as math phobic, afraid of public speaking, or inadequate writers? Once people have convinced themselves that they are incompetent in a domain, it's a struggle for teachers to break that self-imposed stereotype.

It is important to note that when we refer to competence as a prime motivator, we are talking about genuine competence, not the stereotypical illusion of competence in suburban little league games in which everybody gets a trophy and juice box. Students, including those of primary age, know how to keep score and are acutely aware of the differences between their actual performance and what success looks like. The key to using competence as a motivator is what Harvard professor Teresa Amabile calls *The Progress Principle*—allowing people to know that, day by day, they are getting closer to their goal (Hickey 2001). One reason that grades are such a poor motivator is the gap—weeks or months—between the performance of the student and the grade on the report card. Even gaps of days between when work is submitted and the time that the teacher is able to grade papers and hand back the work with a score attached can be an eternity in motivational terms. We have seen kindergarten and first-grade students track their progress in reading on simple bar charts, and students at all grade levels maintain writing portfolios in which they can explain to parents, teachers, and casual observers how their writing has improved since their last attempt.

. . . .

A single error—especially one that is public and embarrassing—can lead to a label that persists for a lifetime.

. . . .

While competence is a great motivator, the value of competence is enhanced significantly when students feel competent at something that matters to them. For example, while improvements in writing are of enormous value to students (Graham 2015), students also thrive on writing for an audience about whom they care deeply. Writing for a school newspaper, website, or literary magazine, with audiences that include parents, relatives, and friends, carries with it a higher value than any classroom assignment we could create. The opportunities to create physical and virtual portfolios that show improvement abound, from YouTube to TikTok to a variety of school-based technology solutions.

• •

The value of competence is enhanced significantly when students feel competent at something that matters to them.

• •

When seeking to provide relevance and personal significance for students to promote their engagement and competence, it is tempting to substitute what adults think is relevant and meaningful for the genuine interests of students. In a classroom dominated by new arrivals to the United States, for example, one of us designed a thoroughly engaging unit that made use of immigration data and the context for a lesson on visual displays of quantitative information in math. But what the students really found relevant and meaningful were units on creating businesses. In another case, we created a splendid unit that focused on sports, when the students were far more engaged in the information that addressed the realities of transgender students, a subject of vital interest to friends and loved ones.

HOW SHAME DESTROYS MOTIVATION

Shame is a profoundly debilitating emotion. Unlike guilt, which is associated with regret for a particular behavior or action, shame is a pervasive feeling of worthlessness that cannot be remedied with improved performance. Once a child or adult feels shame—for being stupid, incompetent, and worthless in the eyes of authority figures—no amount of personal improvement is sufficient to remedy the condition (Barth 2018). While we do not believe that teachers and administrators ever intentionally inflict shame on students and peers, the effects of their actions are unmistakable. Even when the intentions of the teacher are good, the impact on the student can be devastating (Frey and Fisher 2008). Here are some examples:

THE TEACHER INTENDS . . .	THE STUDENT HEARS . . .
"I don't want to call on her because I don't want to embarrass her—she almost always has the wrong answer."	"The teacher never calls on me because I'm stupid—I'll never get any better."
"I'll give Max an A on this assignment—it will make her mom really proud of her."	"Everybody, including my mom, knows I didn't deserve an A. The teacher must think I can't ever do the work in this class."
"Javier has such trouble speaking and writing—I'll let him do a PowerPoint project for this communication assignment and that way he'll be able to meet the standard without having to say or write anything."	"I'm the only kid in the class who gets to do PowerPoint without saying a word? Just because I'm learning English doesn't mean I'm stupid, but the teacher must think I'm hopeless."
"Hey, I was just having a little fun—can't kids these days take a joke?"	"He humiliated me in front of my friends. I acted as if it was okay, but his little joke and daily sarcasm burn a hole straight through me."

Shame-inducing behaviors are not limited to interactions between teachers and students. For years, administrators have engaged in variously labeled inspections of classrooms—learning walks, instructional rounds, or variations on the theme. If these observations are accompanied by meaningful feedback and support, they can be powerful tools for improved teaching and learning. But those constructive observations appear to us to be the exception rather than the rule. More commonly, the observers enter the classroom, watch the lesson, look at the work on the walls, and occasionally talk with a student and then . . . nothing. The feedback to the teacher, if it occurs at all, is filtered through the principal, and days, weeks, or months can pass before the teacher gains any understanding—without the possibility of rejoinder—about what the observers saw. Meanwhile, teachers fill in the silence with their worst fears. "If they thought I was a competent teacher," their fearful reasoning goes, "they would have at least said something."

. . . .

Once shame sets in, it is very difficult to change psychological course.

. . . .

At the senior leadership level, we have seen experienced and dedicated professionals reduced to emotional rubble with an unkind word from a senior leader, peer, board member, or community observer. In a polarized political climate, disagreement is rarely a reasonable divergence of opinion on policy, but rather because the opponent is evil, venal, and unworthy of being an educator. This is not an environment in which learning by adults or students can thrive. The behavior that is most closely related to these actions is bullying—perhaps something that many readers have experienced. Bullies rely not only on physical force but also on emotional intimidation. And while every teacher who has worked on the playground knows that bullying is toxic and wrong, we continue to see classic bullying behavior take place among adults in public forums.

Once shame sets in, it is very difficult to change psychological course. When considering the impact of shame, whether associated with classroom errors, body image, coordination, physical appearance, or addiction of any kind, the remedy is never a cheery pep talk but often years of psychotherapy. The best—indeed, nearly the only—way to reduce shame is to avoid it in the first place. This requires calling out shaming behaviors by students and adults and making it clear that it is a firing offense.

PUTTING THE "L" BACK IN SEL

During the global pandemic and the personal tragedies of lost friends and relatives associated with it, schools recognized that they had a role to play in addressing the trauma experienced by students and staff. This led to an unprecedented emphasis on social and emotional learning. The deaths and illnesses of families, friends, and colleagues are perpetual reminders of how fragile life is and of how the emotional needs of children and adults are a central responsibility of educational leadership. It is therefore understandable that many schools are prioritizing the social and emotional needs of students as they begin the school year in virtual, blended, and on-site learning environments. The question leaders and teachers must face is not whether to give the emotional needs of students priority, but how to do so.

Social and emotional needs of children rest on the twin pillars of safety and identity. Students must be physically safe, with adequate nutrition, freedom from abuse and neglect, and protected to the maximum extent possible from COVID-19. They must also be emotionally safe, with the confidence to seek help without fear, express their needs without embarrassment, and share their joys, sorrows, and apprehensions with a loving and caring adult. In addition, students need a sense of identity—classmates, teachers, and trusted adults who know their names, appreciate their personalities, and engage with them about interests outside of school. That was true before 2020, and it is especially true now.

. . . .

Social and emotional needs of children rest on the twin pillars of safety and identity.

. . . .

But as much as we care deeply about the social and emotional needs of students, some schools are making a grave error when they separate those needs from the "L" in SEL (social and emotional learning). The pursuit of social and emotional development without learning is futile and destructive. As schools reopened in the fall of 2021, we heard a school leader suggest, "For the first few weeks of school, we're not going to worry about academics, but only focus on SEL." This attitude reflects a fundamental misunderstanding of what social and emotional learning is all about. If you want to see elementary school students who are stressed out, full of anxiety, and depressed, then deprive those students of the opportunity to feel competent and successful as learners. To say, "We don't have time for literacy because we need to attend to students' social and emotional needs" is counterproductive and dangerous. If you want to see middle and high school students who are self-destructive and ready to explode, deprive them of social contact and a sense of personal agency for six months, and then, when they are re-entering virtual, blended, or in-person learning environments, tell them that their personal competence doesn't matter as long as they are socially and emotionally well. There are no adolescents on the planet who will be emotionally healthy if they feel incompetent.

Think about it: Why do students retreat into the inner world of video games while they ignore schoolwork? Because with video games, as violent and inappropriate as they might be, the kids know that they are getting better all the time. They keep score, get feedback, improve, and know the objective truth that they are competent. Misguided approaches to social and emotional care that exclude academic success—including assessment, feedback, improvement, and competence— undermine the very emotional health that they seek to attain.

Finally, let us put aside social and emotional learning as a program—a curriculum to march through as if it were the psychological equivalent of flashcards, after which we can say, "Now that this program is done, we can get back to teaching." The very best social and emotional learning includes practices that are imbued in all our interactions with students and adults throughout the day. It is not something done to students, but rather an ethic that pervades interpersonal relationships at every level. It is the respect accorded to students, parents, bus drivers, cafeteria and custodial staff, and every human with whom we come into contact. We know their names, listen before speaking, and value them as humans. And we teach students to read, solve problems, and think not because it might be on the test, but because that is part and parcel of our love and care for them.

To be clear: social and emotional learning is a vital part of every school year. But the focus on the social and emotional needs of students without learning will undermine the psychological health of the students who need us the most.

BARRIERS TO ENGAGEMENT DURING CHALLENGES

Although every teacher understands the value of engagement, there are three institutional barriers that often get in the way of effective engagement. The first is the sheer size of the curriculum, which reflects state standards. Even before the interruptions of learning that occurred during the global pandemic, most teachers found that there were simply too many standards—and the possibility that those standards might be tested on state assessments—for the time available. As a result, teachers were diverted from effective engagement to simply delivering the content as rapidly as possible. Though the idea that delivery without engagement leads to student learning is a concept unburdened by evidence, the prevailing thought in many schools is, "If they miss these items on the state test, it won't be my fault because I can document that I covered it."

The second barrier to engagement is the shrinking number of minutes allocated during the school day to address the same content. Many high schools, for example, have increased the number of periods from five or six to nine to provide more choices to students. The practical effect is that teachers have forty minutes to teach and assess the same curriculum for which they formerly had sixty minutes.

The third barrier to engagement is an emotional one—the reluctance of teachers to put students under too much stress and anxiety that can be associated, in the view of some teachers, with the requirements for student interactions in class. This is exacerbated by the use of anonymous student surveys in which teachers can be savaged by students and threatened by administrators if their ratings reflect student discomfort with being challenged in class.

There are ways leaders can address these barriers, but it requires political will and professional courage to do so. First, district leaders can collaborate with teachers to explicitly reduce the number of standards that are taught. State policy makers are under incessant demands to expand standards by groups who are certain that "every fourth grader should know . . ." and "if you exclude this part of the history curriculum, you are guilty of censorship and omitting vital knowledge our students need." We are not aware of any state that has, in response to these demands, reduced standards in other areas to make room for the additional requirements, extended the school year, or otherwise addressed the reality that the demand for more content in the same number of minutes in the day inevitably leads to superficiality, random omissions of content, and the absence of student engagement.

· ·

District leaders can collaborate with teachers to explicitly reduce the number of standards that are taught.

· ·

Second, leaders can resist the siren call to treat students as customers and give wide choices in a fragmented curriculum. The customer experience of students in their online shopping is one in which immediate gratification is expected and failure to meet the demands of the customer results in the product being returned. But educators are not in the business of instant gratification and that is why, despite the claims of some political leaders, students are not customers. Every veteran educator reading this book has had the experience of students thanking them years later for their high expectations and rigorous demands. In our combined century of teaching experience, we have not had a student thank us for challenge and rigor on the same day the students experienced it.

Finally, leaders must use surveys of students with caution. While there is some evidence that surveys of student engagement offer insights, there is powerful evidence that surveys—including those of students—yield unreliable and demonstrably untrue information (Stephens-Davidowitz 2017).

HOW LEADERS MODEL PERSEVERANCE THROUGH CHALLENGE

Moving from the classroom to the boardroom, the demand for perfection and error-free decisions is even more insidious. "Before we adopt this recommendation," senior leaders and policy makers insist, "you have to prove to me that it will work." These failure-free attitudes persist in the illusion that there is such a thing as ideal decisions in which failure is beyond the realm of possibility. In order to avoid this illusion, leaders and policy makers should insist on the discipline of mutually exclusive decision alternatives (Beshears and Gino 2015; Reeves 2021a).

First, leaders insist that before a decision recommendation is made, there must be at least two mutually exclusive alternatives. This stands in direct contrast to the typical decision process in which the staff will come together and, behind closed doors, vet the alternatives and recommend a single decision to the superintendent and board. This creates the illusion of perfection that is never sufficient. The discipline of mutually exclusive decision alternatives, by contrast, requires that the staff provide at least two alternatives, each of which has clear advantages and disadvantages. This allows the superintendent and other senior leaders and policy makers to make a clear-eyed decision, knowing that however thoroughly vetted the recommendation may be, there are clearly disclosed advantages and disadvantages to the decision they are considering. This discipline is especially essential in areas where there may be limited information dominated by a single person, a phenomenon that we especially see in the areas of technology and finance. In these areas, there is a tendency of senior leaders and policy makers to defer to the expertise of those with a monopoly of information. This can lead to disastrous consequences when leaders and policy makers make decisions based on inadequate information and the illusion that the recommendations they received were without risk. A superior decision discipline is the requirement for alternatives and clearly disclosed advantages and disadvantages.

THE PSYCHOLOGICAL SAFETY IMPERATIVE

If we expect students and adults to learn from mistakes and value errors as part of the learning experience, then leaders must create an environment of psychological safety. Evidence from fields as diverse as education, medicine, aviation, and finance is consistent; when people fear repercussions from mistakes, the result is not the absence of error, but rather the failure to report errors and learn from them (Edmondson 2018). While the rhetoric of educational leadership and pedagogy reflects an understanding of this research, the practical reality is that students and adults frequently lack psychological safety and hence avoid innovation, risk-taking, and the errors that go with trying new ideas and practices (Reeves 2021b). One reason that psychological safety is easier to talk about than model is the widespread misunderstanding about what student engagement looks like in the classroom. When, for example, classroom observations by administrators and other evaluators have ambiguous criteria, the safe course for teachers is to call on students who reliably know the answers or only recognize students whose hands are raised, avoiding the unpleasantness associated with a disappointing wrong answer that might reflect badly on the teacher. After all, if teachers had prepared students well, then the visitors to the classroom will see an orderly group of students who have done their homework, learned their lessons, and are prepared to demonstrate their learning as the administrator watches approvingly. But this scenario is not real engagement, only the illusion of engagement (Gupta and Reeves 2021).

. . . .

The practical reality is that students and adults frequently lack psychological safety and hence avoid innovation, risk-taking, and errors.

. . . .

One of the best tests of psychological safety in the classroom is the use of equity sticks, in which the teacher randomly calls on students by drawing a stick with a name on it out of a jar. While this is commonly done in the primary grades, it is rare in the intermediate and secondary grades. When we ask teachers why they are unwilling to call on students randomly so that there is a true representation of what students already know and what they have yet to learn, the most common explanation is that the teachers don't want to embarrass the students who don't know the answer. This explanation says it all—mistakes are a source of embarrassment and humiliation in those classrooms, not a path to learning. The same dynamic takes place in professional learning sessions in which a facilitator, in order to gain 100% engagement by the participants, will randomly call on participants to share their insights. We have done this frequently but can always count on feedback in which participants object to being put on the spot or embarrassed in front of their colleagues. If we can't get educational professionals to demonstrate the value of psychological safety and learning from error, then the chances of these conditions prevailing in the classroom and staff meetings are remote.

. . . .

The real world is all about making mistakes, getting feedback— from professors, managers, and peers—and then using that feedback to improve the quality of work.

. . . .

Another characteristic of psychological safety is a culture of feedback and, crucially, response to feedback that results in improved performance. Although accurate and timely feedback is a strong predictor of improved student performance (Hattie 2013), many teachers spend an extraordinary amount of time and energy providing feedback that is not used by the students to improve performance. The teachers award a grade and often provide excellent feedback, but then refuse to allow the students to use that feedback to resubmit the work that reflects their application of the feedback. When resubmission of work is allowed, often the first and second submissions are averaged, diminishing the incentive for students to work hard to turn in the best possible work based on the teacher's feedback. These deeply flawed practices are often justified with the explanation that in the real world, one must get things right the first time and that resubmission is not permitted in the cruel reality awaiting students after their graduation. In fact, the real world is all about making mistakes, getting feedback—from professors, managers, and peers—and then using that feedback to improve the quality of work. The authors of this book are relatively well-published writers, yet none of us has ever had the first draft of anything accepted. Our real world, and that of our students, is never about getting it right the first time, but always about receiving feedback, respecting that feedback, and applying that feedback. If editors did not have a psychologically safe environment for writers to make mistakes, then few books would ever be published.

WHAT TEACHERS AND LEADERS CAN DO NOW

In this chapter we considered how to improve engagement as students deal with struggle and failure. We confronted some common misunderstandings about student motivation and social and emotional learning. When students are struggling, challenge is not only possible, but it is an essential for improved learning, student self-confidence, and engagement. In the next chapter we explore how to expand student ownership of their own engagement and learning.

1. Challenge the false rhetoric about failure. If someone talks about how valuable failure is as a learning event, ask directly, "So what happened the last time a student or teacher made a mistake?" Ask if they are willing to give up using the average to evaluate students and adults so that past mistakes are not held against them.

2. Open a discussion about student motivation, including rank-ordering the factors in motivation. If colleagues persist in using grades as motivators, consider a discussion of how many students will have the same school experience and career ambitions as their teachers.

(Continued)

(Continued)

3. Explore the sources of shame in your schools. Attempt candid conversations about when students and adults have been shamed, however unintentionally, and discuss how to avoid that in the future.

4. Discuss your SEL practices and curriculum and consider how learning and student competence and confidence can be an explicit part of that.

5. Discuss the barriers to engagement, including the overwhelming burdens of standards and curriculum and the inadequate amount of time given to teachers for teaching, assessment, and engagement. Consider a pilot project in which some volunteer teachers focus on fewer standards with greater depth and more opportunities for re-teaching and re-assessment when students are struggling.

6. Review your leadership decision-making process. What would be required to move from a take-it-or-leave-it system of a single recommendation to mutually exclusive decision alternatives?

7. Assess the degree of psychological safety in classrooms and professional learning settings. How can you make it safer for students and adults to make mistakes and learn from them?

CHAPTER FOUR

Control

Increase Students' Ownership of Their Own Engagement and Learning

iStock.com/Prostock-Studio

In this chapter, you will learn about . . .

- Cognitive challenges to learning
- Fostering students' ownership of learning

Much has been written about intrinsic motivation, especially the value and impact of intrinsic motivation on engagement and learning (e.g., Meece et al. 2006). It probably is not a surprise that intrinsic motivation facilitates engagement, which in turn facilitates learning. But schools are filled with extrinsic motivations, such as consequences, grades, recognition, and punishments (or even candy, as described in the last chapter). These seem to work in the short term, but when the rewards are gone, the behavior starts to diminish. It seems that many of us do certain things for the reward but stop doing them when the reward is removed.

. . . .

Many of us do certain things for the reward but stop doing them when the reward is removed.

. . . .

Thus, if we want to ensure deep engagement with learning, educators must teach, monitor, and address students' intrinsic motivation. We can do so by increasing students' ownership of their learning. We have already addressed the need to ensure that students see learning as relevant. And we have addressed the value of productive struggle. In this chapter, we turn our attention to the ways in which we can increase students' ownership of the learning process.

In 2016, we noted that there were several factors that helped students assume ownership of their learning (Frey et al. 2018, 2021), including

- Students know their current performance levels.
- Students know what they are expected to learn and have the confidence to engage in the challenge.
- Students select tools to guide their learning.
- Students monitor their progress and make adjustments in their learning.
- Students seek feedback and know that errors are opportunities to learn.
- Students recognize that they have learned and they teach others.

Before we explore these factors of student ownership further, it's important to recognize that there are cognitive barriers to learning. And these barriers can result in disengagement. By understanding the various reasons that students disengage, teachers may be able to take action and address the barriers. In doing so, we may be able to increase students' ownership of learning.

COGNITIVE CHALLENGES TO LEARNING

"Taylor is not motivated." How many times have you heard that about a student? It's an explanation for lack of progress that unfortunately looks past what might be getting in the student's way.

"I taught it. They didn't learn it." That comment betrays an uninformed view of how learning happens. We have long known that a transmission-of-knowledge model, where students passively receive and then reproduce information, is not how learning occurs (Donovan and Bransford 2005).

"They just don't care." That kind of reasoning reflects a lack of understanding about the importance of relevance and purpose for learning as a foundation for building from known knowledge to new knowledge.

Too often we ascribe student barriers to learning in sweeping terms without looking closely at the causes. When we fail to carefully examine the reasons that students disengage, we make it impossible to see what we might do in order to make a positive impact. Better to flip the script and examine them from a different perspective: these are cognitive barriers to effective teaching.

. . . .

Too often we ascribe student barriers to learning in sweeping terms without looking closely at the causes.

. . . .

Chew and Cerbin (2020) drew on extensive research on how students learn and proposed a framework for understanding what might be getting in the way of being able to engage a student effectively. The nine cognitive barriers to learning, as well as sample teaching strategies that aim to overcome them, can be found in Figure 4.1. Of course, there are many more response options; we've just started the list.

Figure 4.1 • Responses to Cognitive Challenges

CHALLENGE	BARRIER	TEACHING APPROACH
1. Student mental mindset	Doesn't see purpose or relevance in the topic Doesn't believe they have the ability to learn the content Has experienced failure in the content before and believes that they do not have the skills necessary to learn	Explain the value and importance of the learning, increase students' ownership of their learning, and teach the habits of minds and mindsets
2. Metacognition and self-regulation	May be overconfident about their knowledge or skills and therefore doesn't devote attention to it May not have the skills to monitor and reflect on learning May not yet have the skills to focus and bring attention back to the task	Create reflection assignments; teach students about planning, monitoring, and adjusting their learning; develop coping strategies to refocus on learning; and use practice tests to identify content that can still be learned
3. Student fear and mistrust	Teacher-student relationship is damaged Student has been bullied or experienced trauma	Focus on teacher credibility (especially the trust students have with the teacher and their belief that they can learn from that teacher), restructure feedback, and create a safe climate for learning and making mistakes
4. Insufficient prior knowledge	Needs prerequisite skills or concepts for mastery of new content are missing	Use initial assessments; provide lessons, background knowledge, and key vocabulary in advance; and use interactive videos

CHALLENGE	BARRIER	TEACHING APPROACH
5. Misconceptions	Possesses misconception about a topic that remains even when exposed to accurate information	Use advance organizers, recognize common misconceptions for students at a specific age or in a specific content area, and invite students to justify their responses to that thinking
6. Ineffective learning strategies	Utilizes sub-optimal learning or study skills Does not have alternative approaches when current strategies do not work	Teach study skills, model effective strategies with think-alouds, and teach about spaced practice
7. Transfer of learning	Can't apply knowledge, skills, or concepts to new or novel situations	Plan appropriate tasks, model application in different contexts, tailor feedback to include processing of the task
8. Constraints of selective attention	Believes they can multitask or focuses on irrelevant stimuli	Increase teacher clarity (students need to know what they are learning and why), use breaks and re-orientation strategies, and teach students to avoid multitasking, especially with media
9. Constraints of mental effort and working memory	Finds task too complex or is trying to memorize too much information	Organize information and chunk it, use both visual and auditory cues (dual coding), and use retrieval practice

Source: Adapted from Fisher and Frey (2021).

Let's take, as an example, a student who is experiencing cognitive overload. The tasks at hand have exceeded the working memory of this particular student and they have withdrawn. If the teacher correctly identified that barrier to learning, the teacher might be able to re-engage the learner by initiating retrieval practice using some of the universal response options noted in Chapter 2 and slowing down to chunk some information for the learner.

In the same class, another student may not have an effective learning strategy. Let's say that the teacher has asked for a written response to a writing prompt. The student gets started with an opening sentence, but then stops working and looks toward the ceiling. When asked, the student says, "I'm trying to think, but I don't know what to write next." In this case, the student may not have an effective strategy for completing the task and does not know what to do. The response would be different from a student experiencing cognitive overload.

In a third example, the student is distracted by peers and does not currently have the skills to bring their mind back to the task. The student had the goal of completing the tasks and was attending to it but does not have the self-regulation skills to refocus. In this case, teaching self-regulation and providing feedback about how the student has processed the task could help the student, over time, to develop self-regulation skills.

As a final example, the student thinks that the teacher does not like them. The evidence they present is the feedback the teacher has given on recent assignments. The student says, "See, this teacher doesn't like me. Just look at my paper. The teacher didn't write like this on other papers." In some cases, students interpret teacher feedback as evidence that the teacher does not like the student and it raises the affective filter, or fear and mistrust of the teacher. In this case, the teacher needs to restructure the feedback and ensure that the environment in the classroom is safe to learn.

These nine cognitive challenges to learning can be used to identify possible reasons that students disengage and direct teachers to actions that they can take to re-engage the learner. Notice that many of the actions are designed to increase students' ownership of learning. We'll focus on doing exactly that in the next section.

FOSTERING STUDENTS' OWNERSHIP OF LEARNING

Students who take ownership of their learning have very specific experiences in their classes. Their teachers are intentional and purposeful about transferring responsibility to students, and simultaneously ensure that there are scaffolds and supports in place for students as needed. Importantly, teachers who see their role as the development of intrinsic motivation and students' ownership of learning plan lessons with these characteristics in mind.

. . . .

For many students, the question "What is learning?" is elusive.

. . . .

Defining Learning

For many students, the question "What is learning?" is elusive. They understand what it means to complete tasks, but many students have not been asked what it means to learn something. Maybe they have taken this for granted or assumed that they learned. And maybe they did learn because they could recall or use their new knowledge. But students need to have the language of learning. So, we encourage you to start by surveying students. It's a great starting point or check-in point for the change in students' experiences with school. You might ask them to reflect on their results or perhaps discuss them. We developed a tool that can be used to engage students in this type of conversation (see Figure 4.2).

Figure 4.2 • What Is Learning?

LESSON

1

What Is Learning?

Learning is a complex process. One thing that greatly impacts your learning is the way that you actually think about learning. Today we are going to explore what is called conceptions of learning. Conceptions of learning are your ideas and beliefs that you have about being a learner.

Conceptions of learning fall into six categories:

① Learning as gaining information

② Learning as remembering, using, and understanding information

③ Learning as a duty

④ Learning as personal change

⑤ Learning as a process not bound by time or place

⑥ Learning as the development of social competence

Think About It

A FUN FACT about Conceptions of Learning

Studies show that your conceptions of learning have a direct correlation, or connection, to your academic achievement. So what you think about learning affects your individual success as a learner! It also affects your motivation as a learner and the strategies you select when you are in the learning process.

Let's dig a little deeper into each of the categories by taking the following survey. You'll take this survey multiple times throughout the school year to see if your conceptions of learning change.

Conceptions of Learning Survey—Time 1

Date: _____

Directions: Read each statement carefully and think about how you feel about yourself as a learner. Check the box that best represents your response to each statement. There are no right or wrong answers. The purpose of this survey is to establish a baseline about what *you* think and feel about learning.

	I think...	Strongly Agree	Agree	Disagree	Strongly Disagree
1	Learning is when I'm taught something that I didn't know before.				
2	Learning is taking in as many facts as possible.				
3	When someone gives me new information, I feel like I am learning.				
4	Learning helps me become clever (quick to understand, learn, apply ideas).				
5	Learning means I can talk about something in different ways.				
6	When something stays in my head, I know I have really learned it.				
7	If I have learned something, it means that I can remember that information whenever I want to.				
8	I should be able to remember what I have learned at a later date.				
9	I have really learned something when I can remember it at a later date.				
10	When I have learned something, I know how to use it in other situations.				
11	If I know something well, I can use the information if the need arises.				
12	Learning is making sense out of new information and ways of doing things.				
13	I know I have learned something when I can explain it to someone else.				
14	Learning is finding out what things really mean.				
15	Learning is difficult but important.				
16	Even when something I am learning is difficult, I must concentrate and keep on trying.				
17	Learning and studying must be done whether I like it or not.				
18	Learning has helped me widen my views about life.				
19	Learning changes my way of thinking.				
20	By learning, I look at life in new ways.				

1   What Is Learning?

	I think...	Strongly Agree	Agree	Disagree	Strongly Disagree
21	Learning means I have found new ways to look at things.				
22	Increased knowledge helps me become a better person.				
23	I use learning to develop myself as a person.				
24	When I learn, I think I can change as a person.				
25	Learning is necessary to help me improve as a person.				
26	I don't think I will ever stop learning.				
27	I learn a lot from talking to other people.				
28	Learning is gaining knowledge through daily experiences.				
29	Learning is knowing how to get along with different kinds of people.				
30	Learning is not only studying at school but also knowing how to be considerate to others.				
31	Learning is the development of common sense in order to become a better member of society.				
32	Learning is developing good relationships.				

Count how many check marks you had for each answer choice, and capture the numbers in the table below.

Strongly Agree	Agree	Disagree	Strongly Disagree
/ 32	/ 32	/ 32	/ 32

As we continue throughout the school year and work to become assessment-capable visible learners, we will return to this survey tool and see if any of your conceptions of learning have changed.

Conceptions of Learning Survey—Time 2

Date: _____

Directions: Read each statement carefully and think about how you feel about yourself as a learner. Check the box that best represents your response to each statement. There are no right or wrong answers. The purpose of this survey is to establish a baseline about what *you* think and feel about learning.

	I think...	Strongly Agree	Agree	Disagree	Strongly Disagree
1	Learning is when I'm taught something that I didn't know before.				
2	Learning is taking in as many facts as possible.				
3	When someone gives me new information, I feel like I am learning.				
4	Learning helps me become clever (quick to understand, learn, apply ideas).				
5	Learning means I can talk about something in different ways.				
6	When something stays in my head, I know I have really learned it.				
7	If I have learned something, it means that I can remember that information whenever I want to.				
8	I should be able to remember what I have learned at a later date.				
9	I have really learned something when I can remember it at a later date.				
10	When I have learned something, I know how to use it in other situations.				
11	If I know something well, I can use the information if the need arises.				
12	Learning is making sense out of new information and ways of doing things.				
13	I know I have learned something when I can explain it to someone else.				
14	Learning is finding out what things really mean.				
15	Learning is difficult but important.				
16	Even when something I am learning is difficult, I must concentrate and keep on trying.				
17	Learning and studying must be done whether I like it or not.				
18	Learning has helped me widen my views about life.				
19	Learning changes my way of thinking.				
20	By learning, I look at life in new ways.				

1 What Is Learning?

	I think...	Strongly Agree	Agree	Disagree	Strongly Disagree
21	Learning means I have found new ways to look at things.				
22	Increased knowledge helps me become a better person.				
23	I use learning to develop myself as a person.				
24	When I learn, I think I can change as a person.				
25	Learning is necessary to help me improve as a person.				
26	I don't think I will ever stop learning.				
27	I learn a lot from talking to other people.				
28	Learning is gaining knowledge through daily experiences.				
29	Learning is knowing how to get along with different kinds of people.				
30	Learning is not only studying at school but also knowing how to be considerate to others.				
31	Learning is the development of common sense in order to become a better member of society.				
32	Learning is developing good relationships.				

Count how many check marks you had for each answer choice, and capture the numbers in the table below.

Strongly Agree	Agree	Disagree	Strongly Disagree
/ 32	/ 32	/ 32	/ 32

Now that you've taken the Conceptions of Learning Survey for the second time this school year, let's look at how these results compare to your results the first time you took the survey.

Conceptions of Learning Survey **Time 1 Results**	Strongly Agree	Agree	Disagree	Strongly Disagree
	/ 32	/ 32	/ 32	/ 32
Conceptions of Learning Survey **Time 2 Results**	Strongly Agree	Agree	Disagree	Strongly Disagree
	/ 32	/ 32	/ 32	/ 32
Time 1 and Time 2 Changes				

Reflect

Were there any changes in the way you responded to the statements in the Conceptions of Learning Survey from the first time you took it to the second time? If so, what were they?

What do you think was the cause of those changes?

1   What Is Learning?

Conceptions of Learning Survey—Time 3

Date: _____

Directions: Read each statement carefully and think about how you feel about yourself as a learner. Check the box that best represents your response to each statement. There are no right or wrong answers. The purpose of this survey is to establish a baseline about what *you* think and feel about learning.

	I think...	Strongly Agree	Agree	Disagree	Strongly Disagree
1	Learning is when I'm taught something that I didn't know before.				
2	Learning is taking in as many facts as possible.				
3	When someone gives me new information, I feel like I am learning.				
4	Learning helps me become clever (quick to understand, learn, apply ideas).				
5	Learning means I can talk about something in different ways.				
6	When something stays in my head, I know I have really learned it.				
7	If I have learned something, it means that I can remember that information whenever I want to.				
8	I should be able to remember what I have learned at a later date.				
9	I have really learned something when I can remember it at a later date.				
10	When I have learned something, I know how to use it in other situations.				
11	If I know something well, I can use the information if the need arises.				
12	Learning is making sense out of new information and ways of doing things.				
13	I know I have learned something when I can explain it to someone else.				
14	Learning is finding out what things really mean.				
15	Learning is difficult but important.				
16	Even when something I am learning is difficult, I must concentrate and keep on trying.				
17	Learning and studying must be done whether I like it or not.				
18	Learning has helped me widen my views about life.				
19	Learning changes my way of thinking.				
20	By learning, I look at life in new ways.				

I think...	Strongly Agree	Agree	Disagree	Strongly Disagree
21	Learning means I have found new ways to look at things.				
22	Increased knowledge helps me become a better person.				
23	I use learning to develop myself as a person.				
24	When I learn, I think I can change as a person.				
25	Learning is necessary to help me improve as a person.				
26	I don't think I will ever stop learning.				
27	I learn a lot from talking to other people.				
28	Learning is gaining knowledge through daily experiences.				
29	Learning is knowing how to get along with different kinds of people.				
30	Learning is not only studying at school but also knowing how to be considerate to others.				
31	Learning is the development of common sense in order to become a better member of society.				
32	Learning is developing good relationships.				

Count how many check marks you had for each answer choice, and capture the numbers in the table below.

Strongly Agree	Agree	Disagree	Strongly Disagree
/ 32	/ 32	/ 32	/ 32

Now that you've taken the Conceptions of Learning Survey for the third time this school year, let's look at how these results compare to your results the second time you took the survey.

Conceptions of Learning Survey **Time 2 Results**	Strongly Agree	Agree	Disagree	Strongly Disagree
	/ 32	/ 32	/ 32	/ 32
Conceptions of Learning Survey **Time 3 Results**	Strongly Agree	Agree	Disagree	Strongly Disagree
	/ 32	/ 32	/ 32	/ 32
Time 2 and Time 3 Changes				

1   What Is Learning?

Reflect

Were there any changes in the way you responded to the statements in the Conceptions of Learning Survey from the second time you took it to the third time? If so, what were they?

What do you think was the cause of those changes?

LESSON 1   What Is Learning?

Teacher Talk

Today we are going to explore what we think about learning and being a learner. The way we are going to do this is through completing what is called a Conceptions of Learning Survey. But before we do, let's talk a little further about what a conception of learning is. Take a look at the top of page 2 in your Learner's Notebook.

Read aloud or have students read to themselves the information that starts at the top of the lesson until they reach the directions for the survey.

So we know now that conceptions of learning are your ideas and beliefs that you have about being a learner. Let's talk a little more about the six categories that conceptions of learning fall into.

It will be important to briefly discuss the six categories of learning to support student understanding.

1. Learning as gaining information
2. Learning as remembering, using, and understanding information
3. Learning as a duty
4. Learning as personal change
5. Learning as a process not bound by time or place
6. Learning as the development of social competence

As the teacher, you can give them the information for each category or you can invite them into a discussion (pairs/groups/class) on what each one is or means and then provide them with additional information. This is a great opportunity to help students understand that learning is so much more than just doing work and "getting a grade." Rather, learning is made up of many different facets and experiences.

After briefly discussing the six categories, let the students know that they will now take the Conceptions of Learning Survey. Make sure they are aware that there are no right or wrong answers—what is most important is that they honestly think about how they feel and what they believe about learning. As they continue to take the survey again at identified intervals throughout the school year, the hope is that through engaging in the lessons included in their *Learner's Notebook* and getting versed in using the tools and checklists in the notebook, their conceptions of learning will begin to change.

Okay, now that we've had time to discuss what conceptions of learning are and the categories your conceptions fall into, we are going to go ahead and take the survey. You need to know that there are absolutely no right or wrong answers to this survey, so as you are individually taking it, answer as honestly as possible. This is not a test. As we continue to engage in the lessons in your Learner's Notebook *and become routine in using the tools and strategies, perhaps your conceptions of learning will change. We will take the survey multiple times throughout the school year to see if that happens. As you are taking the survey, if there is something that you don't understand, please raise your hand and I'd be happy to clarify what the statement is saying.*

Instruct students to go ahead and take the survey.

Now that you've taken the survey, there is one final step you need to complete. At the bottom of the survey there is a small chart. Tally the number of times you selected strongly agree, agree, disagree, or strongly disagree and capture those numbers in the chart.

You will see on the following pages that this survey is designed to be taken several times this year. We will return to it. Today we will stop here and consider this a record of where we are today.

After students have had time to complete the chart, you can bring the lesson to a close.

Student Action

Students will individually take the Conceptions of Learning Survey and complete the chart below it to tally their responses.

Source: Fisher, Frey, Hattie, and Flories (2019c, 2019d).

 Available for download at **resources.corwin.com/crisisofengagement**

Did your students use any verbs to convey their learning, such as *defining* or *analyzing*? Perhaps they believed that learning was about creating or summarizing. Hopefully, they said that they could apply their learning and perhaps even teach others. Increasing students' ownership of their learning requires that we define what it means to learn, and then provide targets for learning each time students are in class.

Ensuring Students Know What They Are Learning and What Success Looks Like

Teacher clarity is an accelerator of students' learning, and we should be thinking about that as we change the environments in which students learn. As part of teacher clarity, it's important that students know what they are learning (learning intentions) and what success looks like (success criteria). We suggest that you are explicit about learning intentions and success criteria for each lesson. The basis of each of these is clarity for learning. We believe that students should be able to answer three questions in each lesson:

1. What am I learning today?

2. Why am I learning it?

3. How will I know that I learned it?

The first question focuses on the learning intentions. What is it that students need to learn today? And *today* is an important consideration. Each day, every day, students should know what they are expected to learn. This requires that teachers understand the standards and how to flow the learning across many days. For example, a student might have the following learning intention: *I am learning about light and how it travels.*

The second question focuses on relevance. Why is this learning important? How will the student use this information in the future? For example, the student learning about light might want to know that they get to design an experiment to conduct with their family and test their parents' knowledge about light. Or they might care that light travels faster than anything else we know of or that light travels in a wave and they will learn about all kinds of different waves.

The third question focuses on success criteria. Note that we did not say "how will my teacher know that I learned it?" but rather "how will *I* know that I learned it?" What might success look like when learning about the travels of light? There are a number of ways that teachers can share success criteria with students. For example, "I can . . ." statements are popular, such as

> I can draw the direction of light travel.
>
> I can explain how light moves.
>
> I can develop an experiment to test light travel using mirrors.

There are other ways to share success, such as with a rubric or with exemplars from other students. Say that students were going to design an experiment about their understanding of light. In that case, success might be measured on a rubric. Or, if they were going to write about it, perhaps some exemplars from previous students would help them.

. . . .

Note that we did not say "how will my teacher know that I learned it?" but rather "how will I know that I learned it"?

. . . .

Importantly, we did not say that students needed to know the answers to these questions at the onset of the lesson, but rather at some point in the lesson, they should know what is expected. We do not think it is fair for students to be required to infer what they are learning. And we do not think it's fair to focus only on the tasks. After all, school is about learning and not just doing things. Given that teachers are required to judge students' learning and record it on report cards or transcripts, clarity of learning seems like the right thing to do. It just doesn't seem right to evaluate the performance of another when they aren't sure what the criteria for success were. And, if you're wondering, students who know what they are learning are significantly more likely to learn it—by about three times. So, let's focus on what students are learning, why it's important, and how they will know that they learned it as we select tools to guide their learning.

· ·

We do not think it is fair for students to be required to infer what they are learning.

· ·

To help students understand these, we have developed lessons that increase students' understanding about where they are going in their learning journey (see Figure 4.3).

Figure 4.3 ♦ Learning Intentions and Success Criteria:
How They Help You Learn

3 Learning Intentions and Success Criteria: How They Help You Learn

TIME:
25 minutes

**ASSOCIATED INFLUENCE
AND EFFECT SIZE:**

Teacher clarity:
0.75

Assessment-capable
visible learners:
1.44

**RELATED TOOLS
AND RESOURCES:**

Learning Intentions
and Success Criteria
Self-Assessment

Overview

This lesson supports students in thinking about the current knowledge and skills that they bring to the "table" with regard to the skills and concepts that will be the focus of the lesson. Students will have an opportunity to think about what they will be learning about for the day and any connections they can make to prior learning experiences. This helps acknowledge what students are already aware of or what they have learned in the past that will support their learning today. It is a good lesson to activate prior background knowledge.

Teacher Preparation

Prior to the Learning Intentions and Success Criteria: How They Help You Learn lesson, you will need to identify the skills and concepts that will be the focus of the lesson, as students will transfer that information into their *Learner's Notebook*.

Teacher Planning Notes:

_____

_____

_____

_____

_____

_____

_____

_____

_____

_____

_____

_____

_____

Learning Intentions and Success Criteria: How They Help You Learn

Think About It

Have you ever been in a class working on an activity but you weren't quite sure **why** you were working on it or **what** you were supposed to be learning?

Was there ever a time when you didn't quite know what you had to do to be successful?

There are a lot of students who would answer **yes** to those questions, which is why we are talking about

learning intentions

and

success criteria.

Learning intentions and success criteria help you know what to do and how your learning is going.

What Are Learning Intentions and Success Criteria?

Learning Intention

A learning intention is what you are supposed to learn after the lesson is over. A learning intention isn't what you are DOING; it is what you are LEARNING.

Success Criteria

There are steps you must take to learn the learning intention, like the steps on a ladder that you climb. These steps are called success criteria.

Let's look at a sample learning intention and success criteria to better understand what they are.

Learning Intention

Today we are learning to describe a character in depth using key details from the story.

Success Criteria

1. I can identify five key details about the character in the story.

2. I can determine what each detail shows about the character.

3. I can use each key detail to describe the character.

How can knowing the

learning intentions and success criteria

for the lesson support your learning?

Reflect

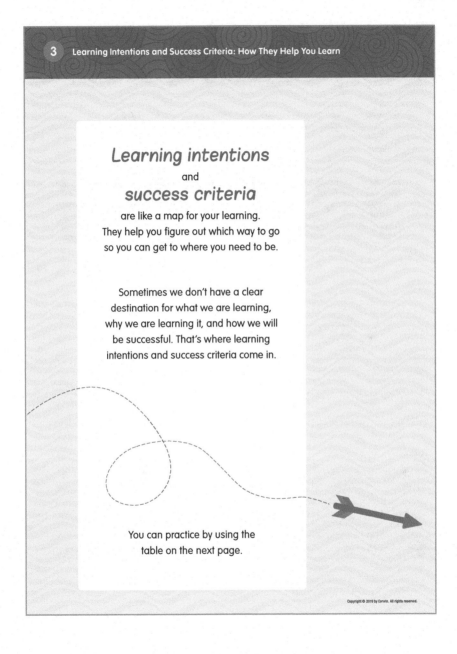

Learning intentions
and
success criteria
are like a map for your learning.
They help you figure out which way to go
so you can get to where you need to be.

Sometimes we don't have a clear
destination for what we are learning,
why we are learning it, and how we will
be successful. That's where learning
intentions and success criteria come in.

You can practice by using the
table on the next page.

Learning Intentions and Success Criteria Self-Assessment

Date: _____

What do you already know?			
What you are learning about today?	I have done this a lot before.	I have done this a little before.	This will be new for me.
1			
2			
3			
4			

Is there anything that doesn't make sense or is unclear to you? Do you know what all of the words mean? Put any questions you have below.

1 **What words or phrases are unclear?**

2 **What do I think they might mean?**

Source: Fisher, Frey, Hattie, and Flories (2019a, 2019b).

 Available for download at **resources.corwin.com/crisisofengagement**

Helping Students Monitor Their Progress

Helping students take responsibility for their learning starts with ensuring students think about what learning means, understand what they are learning, and know how they might know when they have learned it. Those are important starts, but they are just a start on the journey to student owner-ship. The next step focuses on helping students monitor their progress.

Let's not forget the power of helping students monitor their learning so that they know how much of the gap has closed between what they need to know (learning intentions) and where they are now. The success criteria communicate the final destination. But how will students know the stopping points along the way? In other words, how will they know if they are on the right path toward proficiency?

Self-assessment tools can be very useful in helping students monitor their progress. In addition, self-assessment tools provide students an opportunity to reflect on their learning, building some metacognitive skills in the process. It may be that you want to add a self-assessment tool for each chunk of learning that students need to do. They could even use this as a checklist as the learning progresses. For example, the tools shown in Figure 4.4 can help students self-assess so that they can monitor their progress.

Figure 4.4 ◆ Using Success Criteria to Monitor Your Progress

Using Success Criteria to Monitor Your Progress

6

Overview

This lesson provides students with a tool to monitor and evaluate their progress toward the targeted success criteria and also asks students to think about the evidence that they would use to determine where they are in their learning. Like many of the other tools and resources in the *Learner's Notebook*, this is a tool that students can use and apply on a continuous basis until it becomes automatic that they are constantly thinking about where their performance is and what their next learning steps are moving forward. This lesson also supports students in internalizing the success criteria and gaining a deep understanding of what it means and looks like.

Teacher Preparation

Prior to this lesson, create your success criteria and make them visible to students so that they can easily transfer them to their notebooks. Be sure that there are links between the skills embedded in the learning tasks that students will engage in and the success criteria so that they can support where students rate themselves with proper evidence.

Teacher Planning Notes:

TIME:
15 minutes

**ASSOCIATED INFLUENCE
AND EFFECT SIZE:**

Teacher clarity: **0.75**

Self-regulation
strategies: **0.52**

Assessment-capable
visible learners: **1.44**

**RELATED TOOLS
AND RESOURCES:**

Self-Assessing Your
Progress Using
Success Criteria
Template

Using Success Criteria to Monitor Your Progress

In order to become an assessment-capable visible learner, you need to be able to self-assess your learning. Learning intentions and success criteria for a lesson are tools you can use to self-assess. Today, we are going to use a self-assessment tool to help you track your progress using the lesson's success criteria. We will continue to use this tool to self-assess your progress throughout the school year.

6 Using Success Criteria to Monitor Your Progress

Self-Assessing Your Progress Using Success Criteria

Date: _____

Directions: Capture the success criteria for the learning intention provided by your teacher in the boxes below. Prior to the end of the lesson, self-assess your progress by determining your performance level for each success criterion below.

	I'm a pro and can teach others.	I'm able to do this on my own.	I'm still practicing but almost there.	I need more help.
SUCCESS CRITERIA 1:				

Evidence to support current performance level:

My next learning steps:

| **SUCCESS CRITERIA 2:** | | | | |

Evidence to support current performance level:

My next learning steps:

Using Success Criteria to Monitor Your Progress   6

	I'm a pro and can teach others.	I'm able to do this on my own.	I'm still practicing but almost there.	I need more help.
SUCCESS CRITERIA 3:				

Evidence to support current performance level:

My next learning steps:

SUCCESS CRITERIA 4:				

Evidence to support current performance level:

My next learning steps:

Source: Fisher, Frey, Hattie, and Flories (2019c, 2019d).

 Available for download at **resources.corwin.com/crisisofengagement**

Selecting Tools to Guide Learning

There is no one right way for students to learn things. In some classrooms, teachers require that students engage in learning in ways that are most effective and efficient for the teacher. In other classrooms, teachers show students many ways to learn and allow students to identify tools that work for them. Want to guess which group learns more? Given our heading for this section, it should be obvious that students need to be exposed to a wide range of learning and study tools and then be encouraged to choose and use them.

There should be a link between teaching and learning. Of course, we recognize that sometimes that link is broken. But ideally, the tools that are used for teaching impact students' learning. And if we want students to take responsibility for their learning, we need to allow them opportunities to select tools that work for them. We did not say that teachers should provide an endless list of tools, but rather that teachers can provide students with some choices in the selection of tools that will help their learning.

. . . .

And if we want students to take responsibility for their learning, we need to allow them opportunities to select tools that work for them.

. . . .

Let's take graphic organizers as a simple example. At the start of the year, you might introduce students to a range of types. For example, there are many ways to visually represent comparing and contrasting. When students have been taught these ways, they can then have opportunities to select from those tools when the time comes. Of course, they may make a bad choice and then have an opportunity to learn more about the strategic selections of learning tools.

Study skills is another area in which there are many choices. There are a lot of right ways to study, and probably some wrong ways. Students can be provided choices in terms of their study habits once they understand the options that are available. As students make choices, they are developing their skills and become assessment-capable visible learners. And they are much more likely to teach themselves in the future as a result.

In Figure 4.5, you'll find tools that introduce students to various learning tools and ways to get them thinking about which of them would be useful.

Figure 4.5 ◆ Selecting the Right Strategies to Help You Learn

LESSON

8

Selecting the Right Strategies to Help You Learn

There are many different strategies that you can apply to your learning, but knowing what strategy to use and when to use it is critical. When selecting a strategy to support you in your learning, it's important to think about a couple of things. First, you need to know the purpose of your learning. Why are you doing what you are doing? When you know the purpose, it can help you better select appropriate learning strategies. For example, if you know that you are going to be conducting an experiment in your science class, then planning for the task is an effective strategy to select. It is critical for you to be aware of the steps of the experiment, have the supplies and resources that you need, and know the criteria to carry out each step in the experiment. Taking a moment to plan for the task, either individually or with a group of your peers, will help ensure the experiment is carried out safely and effectively.

Directions: Take a moment to look through the strategies below. Think about your understanding of each strategy and what it looks like in your learning. Rate each strategy using the following scale:

❶ I fully understand this strategy and know how to apply it in my learning.

❷ I know what this strategy is, but I'm not sure how to use it in my learning.

❸ I have seen or heard of this strategy before, but I'm not sure what it means or how to use it in my learning.

❹ This is a new strategy for me. I don't know what that looks like.

____ Note-taking	____ Annotating	____ Self-questioning
____ Outlining	____ Repeated reading	____ Self-monitoring
____ Graphic organizers	____ Summarizing	____ Planning for the task
____ Concept mapping	____ Organizing notes	____ Transforming information
____ Synthesizing information	____ Deconstructing information	____ Studying

Let's look at a couple of other examples of learning experiences and determine a strategy that could help support it.

Matching Strategies with Learning Tasks

Directions: Take a moment to read the description of each sample learning task. Then, in the space provided, write your thoughts about which strategy may be effective and why.

1 Sample Learning Task 1:

The bell just rang for social studies class to begin, and your teacher lets you know that in today's lesson you will be exploring all the different causes and effects of World War I. The teacher is going to give a fifteen-minute lecture providing background information about World War I, and then you will be responsible for reading two different primary sources about the war. There are a lot of details to remember that you will need later in order to determine and support your explanation for the causes and effects of World War I.

What might be an effective strategy to use for this learning task?

Why is it an effective strategy?

2 Sample Learning Task 2:

For the past two days in class you have been learning about all the pieces included in an effective argumentative essay, and now you need to start thinking about the design of your own argumentative essay. You can choose from a few options of texts and topics to use for your essay, so you need to figure out how to get started. Before you turn in a final essay, you'll need to submit a rough draft to your teacher. You'll have class time to work on this, but you'll also need to spend some time on this essay outside of class.

What might be an effective strategy to use for this learning task?

Why is it an effective strategy?

Now that you've taken a look at a couple of sample learning tasks, let's focus on what you are learning today and what strategies can support your learning.

8   Selecting the Right Strategies to Help You Learn

 Learning Strategies Checklist

Date: _____

Directions: Think about what you are learning today. Check the boxes that most closely reflect your learning task.

Today your task entails...

Writing an essay/paper

Reading an article

Studying a novel

Conducting an experiment

Working (collaboratively) in a group

Solving problems

Giving a presentation

Taking an assessment/ test/quiz

Learning a new concept or idea

Analyzing data

Analyzing ideas, concepts and/or characters

Creating a project

Evaluating ideas, concepts and/or characters

Writing a lab report

Developing a timeline

Other

Directions: Look at the list of strategies below. Check at least one strategy that you will use to support you in what you are learning today.

Learning Strategies

Note-taking

Outlining

Graphic organizer

Concept mapping

Synthesizing information

Annotating

Repeated reading

Summarizing

Organizing notes

Deconstructing information

Self-questioning

Self-monitoring

Planning for the task

Transforming information

Studying

Selecting the Right Strategies to Help You Learn   8

Did it Work?

Take a moment to think about the strategy you used in your learning today. Why did you select this strategy? Do you think that it supported you in your learning? Why or why not?

Source: Fisher, Frey, Hattie, and Flories (2019c).

 Available for download at **resources.corwin.com/crisisofengagement**

Soliciting Feedback

Feedback works when it is received. That's logical, right? Have you ever given someone feedback and noticed, by the look on their face, that the feedback was not getting through? When that happens, not much change is likely. Our learners are the same. The feedback has to be received if it is to work. And when it is received, good things can happen in terms of students' learning.

The question, then, is how to ensure that feedback is received. To our thinking, the likelihood of feedback being received increases when the learner asks for it. Have you ever asked for feedback from someone? If you were authentic and the feedback was constructive, you probably learned from the experience. Both of these conditions are important. First, the request has to be authentic, and second, the feedback needs to be constructive.

. . . .

The likelihood of feedback being received increases when the learner asks for it.

. . . .

So, we've been teaching students how to solicit feedback rather than wait passively for it. In some classrooms, students simply turn over a card. One side of the card says "working" and the other side says, "feedback needed." In Figure 4.6, we focus on teaching students to how to ask for feedback.

Figure 4.6 • Is It Time for Feedback?

9 | Is It Time for Feedback?

TIME:

20 minutes for
overview of checklists

**ASSOCIATED INFLUENCE
AND EFFECT SIZE:**

Metacognitive
strategies:
0.60

Feedback:
0.70

Help seeking:
0.72

Assessment-capable
visible learners:
1.44

**RELATED TOOLS
AND RESOURCES:**

Is It Time for
Feedback? Checklist

Overview

This lesson is a set up to support students in seeking feedback from themselves, peers, or the teacher. There are prompts to the student that will help structure thinking about what kind of feedback they need and who could be a support in providing it. The goal is to equip students with self-talk and strategies that drive their own ability to provide themselves with feedback or effectively seek it from a peer before immediately going to the teacher, which is what so many students do. In order for these actions to become ingrained in students, the feedback checklists will need to be a routine component of learning.

Teacher Preparation

Students may need support understanding how to use the checklists in the lesson. Examples connected to their current class may support their understanding. It will also be important that the lessons selected for using these checklists lend themselves to students seeking feedback on their own, from a peer or from the teacher.

Teacher Planning Notes:

_____

_____

_____

_____

_____

_____

_____

_____

_____

_____

_____

_____

_____

Feedback is like advice you receive to let you know how you are doing as a learner. The goal of feedback is to help you understand what you need to do in order to get to where you need to be in your learning.

Sometimes you can give yourself the feedback that you need, and other times you may require the help of a peer or the teacher.

Assessment-capable visible learners have different ways to get feedback and know what to do with it.

Here are checklists you can use to help you determine when you need feedback. You will explore ways that you can give yourself feedback or get feedback from a peer or the teacher.

9   Is It Time for Feedback?

Is It Time for Feedback? Checklist

Date: _____

I Can't Get Started in My Learning

What can I do on my **own**?	☐ I can reread the directions to make sure I didn't miss something.
	☐ I can review the success criteria.
	☐ I can use any resources given to me for help.
What can I do with a **peer**?	☐ I can ask my peer to explain what we should be doing.
	☐ I can share the question I have with a peer to see if they could help.
	☐ I can ask my peer to show me how they got started.
What can I do with the **teacher**?	☐ I can make sure I understand what I am supposed to be doing.
	☐ I can walk through an example with the teacher.
	☐ I can ask the teacher to support me in getting started.

Is It Time for Feedback? **9**

I Got Started, But I'm Not Sure Where to Go Next in My Learning

What can I do on my own?
- ☐ I can review the success criteria.
- ☐ I can determine what I got right so far and why.

What can I do with a peer?
- ☐ I can make sure I understand what I am supposed to be working on.
- ☐ I can show my work to my peer and ask for help where I am stuck.
- ☐ I can ask a peer what they think I have gotten right so far and why.

What can I do with the teacher?
- ☐ I can make sure I understand what I am supposed to be doing.
- ☐ I can ask for support in figuring out what to do next.
- ☐ I can ask the teacher to explain the part I am stuck with.

I'm Finished With My Learning

What can I do on my own?
- ☐ I can self-assess my work using the success criteria.
- ☐ I can identify where I have strengths in my work.
- ☐ I can identify where I could get better in my work.

What can I do with a peer?
- ☐ I can ask a peer if they agree I met the success criteria.
- ☐ I can ask a peer to find a strength in my work.
- ☐ I can ask my peer to show me where I could get better in my work.

What can I do with the teacher?
- ☐ I can ask my teacher if they agree I met the success criteria.
- ☐ I can ask my teacher to find a strength in my current work.
- ☐ I can ask my teacher to find a place I could get better in my work.

Source: Fisher, Frey, Hattie, and Flories (2019a, 2019b).

 Available for download at **resources.corwin.com/crisisofengagement**

In addition, we need to teach students to ask questions to get the feedback they need. It's more than "can you help me" or "I don't understand this." Instead, it's learning to ask the right question that will move learning forward. Consider the following feedback frames that can be used to teach students to ask for feedback and to receive that feedback.

GIVING	RECEIVING
I noticed that. . . .	I appreciate you noticing that. . . .
I wondered about. . . .	I hadn't thought about that. . . .
I was confused by. . . .	I heard you say that _____ confused you.
I suggest that. . . .	Based on your suggestion, I will. . . .
Have you thought about . . . ?	Thank you. What would you do?
You might consider. . . .	I'm not sure what that looks like; tell me more.

But this will not work if students are not in a classroom where errors are framed and celebrated as learning opportunities. As we said previously, when students feel embarrassed, shame, or humiliated for making errors, they hide their misunderstandings or check out of the learning. Thus, we emphasize the importance of clearly communicating that we all make errors and that, when we do, it's a chance to learn. The tools in Figure 4.7 can help us teach students that errors are opportunities to learn.

Figure 4.7 ✦ Seeing Errors as Opportunities to Learn

Seeing Errors as Opportunities to Learn

12

Overview

This lesson is designed to help students evaluate their performance and see that errors made in their learning present opportunities to learn moving forward. This works if they take the time to stop and evaluate what may have caused that error and what learning is needed to close the gap.

In this lesson, students will use assessment results from an assessment selected by the teacher and evaluate both the easy and difficult questions they got incorrect and why. It is important that the students be allowed to deem which questions were easy and which were hard instead of being told which category questions fall into. An easy question for one student may prove to be a difficult question for another student, so it is important for each student to determine the difficulty of questions for themselves.

Teacher Preparation

You will need assessment results for students to engage in the learning in the lesson. Possibilities include pre- or postassessment data, unit exam data, quiz data, scoring guide data, and so on.

There are many possibilities in terms of the data to use, but a key variable is that student performance has opportunity for growth. For example, you don't want to use data where all kids earned a perfect score. It is also important to consider the learning opportunities that will be available to students moving forward so that they can close any gaps identified in the data.

Students may also need guidance on what criteria they should use to know if a question was easy or hard for them. Perhaps a way to simplify it is to say that easy questions didn't require a whole lot of thinking on your part while hard questions required you to stop and think about it for a minute.

Teacher Planning Notes:

TIME:
30 minutes

ASSOCIATED INFLUENCE AND EFFECT SIZE:

Self-efficacy: **0.92**

Self-concept: **0.41**

Assessment-capable visible learners: **1.44**

RELATED TOOLS AND RESOURCES:

Reflecting on Errors as Opportunities to Learn Template

Seeing Errors as Opportunities to Learn

Think About It

Stop and think about a time when you made a mistake or an error. It doesn't have to be an example connected to school; it can be anything. You could have been drawing, singing, playing a sport, cooking, talking, skateboarding. Any experience will work that you can think of when you made an error. How did you feel about it? Why did you feel that way? How did you move forward?

Becoming an assessment-capable visible learner means that you can look at the errors you make in your learning as opportunities to grow and build on. Today you are going to look at recent assessment results and use the chart on the next page to self-assess your performance. You will then use your errors to identify areas for growth moving forward.

12 Seeing Errors as Opportunities to Learn

 Reflecting on Errors as Opportunities to Learn

Date: _____

Directions: Read and review the questions on your assessment. As you go through each one, place the question number in one of the four quadrants below.

Questions that I thought were
EASY that I got **WRONG**

Questions that I thought were
HARD that I got **WRONG**

Questions that I thought were
EASY that I got **RIGHT**

Questions that I thought were
HARD that I got **RIGHT**

Seeing Errors as Opportunities to Learn   12

Questions that I thought were EASY that I got WRONG

Question #:   Why did you get it wrong?

What do you need to learn to get it right next time?

Question #:   Why did you get it wrong?

What do you need to learn to get it right next time?

Question #:   Why did you get it wrong?

What do you need to learn to get it right next time?

Question #:   Why did you get it wrong?

What do you need to learn to get it right next time?

12 Seeing Errors as Opportunities to Learn

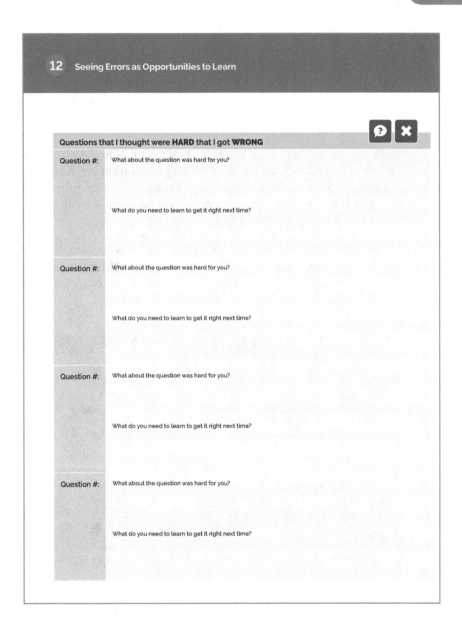

Source: Fisher, Frey, Hattie, and Flories (2019c, 2019d).

 Available for download at **resources.corwin.com/crisisofengagement**

Recognizing Learning

When students assume responsibility for their learning, they recognize when they have learned something. Teachers can use self-questioning to guide students' understanding of their learning. The ability to query one's own understanding is a metacognitive strategy that assists in a learner's ability to self-regulate. There's great value in self-questioning, as it can be the catalyst needed for monitoring one's own learning and making adjustments accordingly. The more we can move students to active decision making about their own learning, the more ownership they have in their learning.

A simple way to encourage self-questioning is to turn "I can" statements into "Can I . . . ?" statements. Consider the following statements that can be modified for students to learn to self-question.

I CAN	CAN I . . . ?
I can name two words that rhyme.	Can I name two words that rhyme?
I can count forward by fives.	Can I count forward by fives?
I can explain what the bar graph tells me about my data.	Can I explain what the bar graph tells me about my data?
I can discuss examples of muscular strength and muscular endurance with my group.	Can I discuss examples of muscular strength and muscular endurance with my group?
I can describe how the tempo can change the mood or emotion of a piece of music.	Can I describe how the tempo can change the mood or emotion of a piece of music?
I can draw a map using map symbols.	Can I draw a map using map symbols?
I can explain how to change water into different states of matter.	Can I explain how to change water into different states of matter?

Of course, self-questioning is more than asking "Can I . . . ?" questions. Additional tools for helping students develop a habit of self-questioning can be found in Figure 4.8.

Figure 4.8 • Using Self-Questioning to Guide Your Learning

Using Self-Questioning to Guide Your Learning

11

Overview

This lesson is set up to support students in asking themselves the right questions to guide their learning throughout the learning process. The template provided for students has them apply self-questioning at three phases of their learning: before the lesson, during the lesson, and after the lesson. Asking students to think about the learning intention and what they already know about it, want to know about it, and need to know about it whets their minds into creating radar for what it is they need to learn as a result of engaging in the learning tasks for the lesson.

Teacher Preparation

Students may need support understanding potential responses to some of the self-questioning for before, during, and after the lesson.

The students will need to have access to the learning intention so they can capture it in their notebook.

Students will most likely not answer the during the lesson questions without prompting to do so, so it would be helpful to have preidentified times during the lesson where you will guide them to do so.

Teacher Planning Notes:

_____

_____

_____

_____

_____

_____

_____

_____

_____

_____

_____

TIME:
15–20 minutes (broken into three chunks)

ASSOCIATED INFLUENCE AND EFFECT SIZE:

Metacognitive strategies:
0.60

Self-verbalization and self-questioning:
0.55

Assessment-capable visible learners:
1.44

RELATED TOOLS AND RESOURCES:

Using Self-Questioning to Guide Your Learning

Self-questioning

happens when you come
up with questions to ask
yourself during different
parts of your learning.

Asking yourself questions
before, during, and **after**
your learning tasks is a strategy
you can use to help yourself
develop as an assessment-
capable visible learner.

In this section, you will practice
using self-questioning.

Using Self-Questioning to Guide Your Learning

Date: _____

Before the Lesson

What am I learning today? What is the learning intention?

What do I already know about this?

What do I want to know about this?

What do I need to do or find out?

During the Lesson

What am I finding out?

What questions do I have as I'm learning?

What is confusing to me?

What do I still need to find out?

After the Lesson

What did I learn as a result of the lesson?

What is still confusing or challenging for me?

What do I still need to practice with?

Source: Fisher, Frey, Hattie, and Flories (2019a, 2019b).

Available for download at **resources.corwin.com/crisisofengagement**

Ideally, students who own their learning take responsibility to teach others. After all, when you teach someone else, you get a chance to learn it again. Cross-age and within-class peer tutoring have a significant impact on student learning, provided that students have moved beyond the surface level of learning in the content they're tutoring. And peer tutoring is an effective way to facilitate the transfer of learning for students. That's why it is an important part of developing ownership in learning for students. We want to be part of schools and classrooms in which students are provided opportunities to show what they have learned by teaching people who still need to learn it. Over time, and with practice, we have seen students who have had peer tutoring opportunities become their own teachers and take responsibility for additional learning.

. . . .

When you teach someone else, you get a chance to learn it again.

. . . .

Imagine classrooms in which these habits are fully realized. Engagement, right? The impact could be amazing, and students might just like school a little bit better.

WHAT TEACHERS AND LEADERS CAN DO NOW

1. Engage with the cognitive challenges to learning and start to identify reasons that students disengage.

2. Develop additional actions that teachers can take to address the cognitive challenges to learning.

3. Increase teacher clarity in every lesson such that students know what they are learning, why they are learning it, and how they will know that they learned it.

4. Teach a range of tools and strategies and allow students to make choices.

5. Develop feedback and monitoring tools such that students increase their self-assessment and self-questioning responsibilities.

6. Develop teach-back and peer tutoring experiences for students to recognize when they have learned something.

CHAPTER FIVE

Collaboration

Consolidating Understanding With Others

iStock.com/fizkes

In this chapter, you will learn about . . .

- Engagement and professional learning
- The collaboration illusion
- Listen—just listen
- How collaboration helps students
- Leading for collaboration and engagement

Collaboration is difficult—just ask any couple you know who has been married for 50 years or more. Or, for that matter, any couple who has been dating for two weeks or more. Collaboration is easy when we overlook the faults of our partners, when we forgive every misstep, and when we always give the best interpretation of our partner's every action. But after a few weeks or a few decades, collaboration becomes far more challenging. In this chapter, we consider the imperative of collaboration on professional learning. However difficult professional collaboration may be, it is one of the greatest incentives—even greater than monetary incentives—to help teachers and leaders in our profession (Reeves 2018).

This chapter begins with the impact of collaboration on professional learning. While it would save our egos to think that teachers and administrators learn best from our keynotes, books, and seminars, the reality is that they learn a lot from one another. We then confront the collaboration illusion—the contrived exercises designed to make people think that they are collaborating when, in fact, they are simply in proximity to one another. We then offer a challenge—to listen, just listen. We have conducted seminars in which we ask people to just listen, without any interruption, commentary, or even affirmation—to just listen—for two, three, or four minutes. Most people find it nearly impossible.

. . . .

The evidence is clear that effective collaboration saves time for teachers.

. . . .

As educators, we are deeply invested in our identities as communicators, and too often that means talking rather than listening. In the context of collaboration, we want to make contributions. Yet time is a zero-sum game—every moment of one person's speaking is another person's lost opportunity to speak. However difficult true collaboration may be, the evidence is clear that collaboration among teachers not only helps their professional learning but also helps students. Specifically, teacher collaboration leads to more consistent and clear feedback, and effective feedback leads to higher levels of student learning (Donahoo, Hattie, and Fells 2018). Time is a finite resource, and therefore, we often hear that teachers do not have the time to invest in collaborative efforts when there are so many other demands in their schedule. Nevertheless, the evidence is clear that effective collaboration saves time for teachers. In particular, collaborative scoring dramatically reduces the time required to assess student work, especially on the time-consuming task of reviewing performance assessments and student writing assignments (Reeves 2020c). The chapter concludes with guidelines for how leaders can support collaboration and how they can avoid the common mistakes that undermine teacher collaboration.

ENGAGEMENT AND PROFESSIONAL LEARNING

To create an engaging classroom environment, teachers need the tools and the practice to nurture and maintain engagement. Having a staff meeting in which one person lectures about the importance of engagement, while tolerating no interaction or engagement by the staff, leads to cognitive dissonance that signals to teachers that collaboration may sound nice, but in practice, it's all about delivery, delivery, and more delivery. In every adult learning opportunity, we must model the levels of engagement—and the practices that lead to engagement—that we expect to see in the classroom. For example, if the expectation is universal participation, including such techniques as think time, whiteboards, and support for peers, then that should be the rule in team meetings of teachers and administrators.

. . . .

In every adult learning opportunity, we must model the levels of engagement—and the practices that lead to engagement— that we expect to see in the classroom.

. . . .

THE COLLABORATION ILLUSION

Professional learning communities (PLCs) are one of the most influential ideas in global education. The central idea is that teaching and learning improve when teachers systematically share their success and challenges and address the following questions (Fisher et al. 2019):

Where are we going?

Where are we now?

How do we move learning forward?

What did we learn?

Who benefited and who did not?

While many schools and educational organizations have claimed the nomenclature of PLCs, their actual practices diverge from the essentials of professional learning in a way best described as "PLC Lite" (DuFour and Reeves 2016). Collaboration is an illusion when it is merely a slot on the schedule, but the substance of a focus on learning, assessment, intervention, and enrichment is not part of the professional conversation.

There are four underlying causes of the collaboration illusion: Avoidance of student achievement data, reluctance to compare teaching practices, fear of evaluation, and the mental and physical exhaustion teachers and administrators face in the aftermath of school closings associated with the global pandemic.

Avoidance of Student Achievement Data

Decades of research support the positive impact of teacher collaboration on the school community and student achievement (Reeves 2020a; Reeves and Eaker 2020). But this research, including international perspectives from an analysis of PISA (Programme for International Student Assessment) scores, has an important caveat: collaboration only has a positive impact when teachers actually discuss student achievement data (Gregorio Mora-Ruano, Heine, and Gebhardt 2019). However obvious this finding may be, we continue to be surprised that much of the time devoted to collaborative teacher meetings is devoted toward subjects far afield of achievement.

. . . .

Collaboration only has a positive impact when teachers actually discuss student achievement data.

. . . .

Whether they are labeled professional learning communities or another variation on the theme, we find these gatherings too frequently are little more than another staff meeting, dominated by an administrator or teacher-leader, focused on logistics and schedules, and other administrative matters. Even when local and state policies are explicit about the work of these meetings (such as Ohio's statewide commitment to "teacher-based teams") and when policies require these teams to specifically address student learning, our review of hundreds of these meetings, along with minutes and other documents, reveals that an explicit focus on student achievement data is the exception rather than the rule. Even when student assessment data is the subject of discussion, most commonly the entire grade level or school is the unit of analysis rather than individual classrooms.

Reluctance to Compare Teaching Practices

Part of this avoidance is the deep cultural reluctance of teaching professionals to compare themselves to one another. As one teacher said about her refusal to list separate data for each teacher, "that would feel evaluative." The way student data is discussed matters—what teacher evaluation expert Kim Marshall calls the difference between discussing teaching rather than teachers. The former is a consideration of practices, while the latter feels like a personal and professional assault (Marshall 2018). We have insisted that these meetings must be a treasure hunt, not a witch hunt, but the threat of humiliation looms large even when teachers are protected by tenure and there are explicit agreements not to use data for evaluative purposes.

Fear of Evaluation

Teachers have reason to be skeptical of these assurances. In the aftermath of the No Child Left Behind Act, many states and school districts embraced Value-Added Evaluation, a statistical model that sought to estimate the impact of individual teachers on student achievement through an analysis of scores on annual state tests. Putting aside the dubious assumption that a single test can measure a year's worth of teaching, the method itself has been discredited and successfully challenged in court (Paige and Amrein 2020). Nevertheless, some states and districts continue to use this method to evaluate teachers, placing a cloud over the credibility of even the legitimate use of student achievement data.

Mental and Physical Exhaustion

Finally, as schools reopened in the aftermath of the global pandemic, the mental and physical exhaustion suffered by teachers and administrators has led to collaborative meetings to focus on student discipline, mental health, and the stress and anxiety of staff members during and after the pandemic. The shortage of substitute teachers and a growing national teacher shortage have led many school leaders to convert planning periods and other scheduled collaborative time to covering classes, with both building administrators and central office staff covering classrooms that otherwise would lack any adult presence. No matter how compelling the case for collaboration is, the safety imperative for adult supervision takes precedence over every other priority. The shortage was severe before the pandemic and is dramatically worse in its aftermath, with almost half of teachers reporting that they are considering leaving the profession in early 2022 (Kiml 2022). It's a catch-22, with teachers citing the absence of collaboration and professional learning as one of the reasons that they are dissatisfied with their jobs (Reeves 2018), yet those are the practices that are cut as the shortage grows worse.

. . . .

Teachers cite the absence of collaboration and professional learning as one of the reasons that they are dissatisfied with their jobs.

. . . .

How can schools overcome the pervasive resistance to meaningful collaboration and the illusions that follow? First, we must recognize that effective collaboration requires practice, the development of inductive reasoning skills, and vulnerability. Certainly, the number of schools that practice effective collaboration is evidence that it can be done, and that these skills can be learned and applied in a matter of months. But to persist through this learning curve, teachers need support and perhaps appropriate incentives. By "incentives," we do not mean merely economic rewards, though teachers surely deserve to be fairly compensated for work, including extra meetings and time devoted to collaborative work. Moreover, incentives for students and staff members can be appropriate and effective to get through the initial stages when the work is difficult and the temptation to give up is strong. While intrinsic motivation is clearly the long-term goal for students and staff members, the evidence from the University of Chicago (List 2022) and elsewhere suggests that intrinsic/extrinsic choice is a false dichotomy and that extrinsic reward can be a bridge to intrinsic motivation. Why? Because the greatest long-term sources of intrinsic motivation are *competence*—the sense that we are good at something—and *efficacy*, the sense that our work has an impact (Donohoo et al. 2018). We do not want to leave the discussion of incentives without noticing that the evidence on adult engagement directly influences teacher satisfaction. Rewards that are meaningful include, for example:

- **Consistent respect for teacher time.** There are no announcements or downtime in meetings, but rather a focus on allowing teachers to get real work done.

- **Safe zones for comment, skepticism, and respectful dissent.** Everyone is valued, even when they disagree. This is the essential insight from the research in environments from the operating room to an aircraft cockpit—without a psychologically safe environment in which challenges are welcome, tragedies happen (Edmondson 2018).

- **Physically safe environments.** This includes lights in parking lots and unambiguous support for teachers who find themselves in a physically unsafe classroom situation.

- **Empathy.** We know superintendents and senior district officials who do more than observe classrooms—they teach full class periods or full days—allowing the classroom teacher to observe a colleague or engage in professional learning. As one superintendent told us, "It's easy to forget how physically and mentally demanding the job of the kindergarten teacher is until you've done about 60 deep knee bends in an hour without a bathroom break."

LISTEN—JUST LISTEN

While the absence of structure can lead teacher meetings to be unproductive, too much structure can lead to a monotonous exercise in completing forms without gaining vital insights into teaching and learning. Administrators and others facilitating collaborative meetings need to recall that communication is not merely about presenting information and sharing insights, but about listening. Elle Allison Napolitano conducts listening exercises with school leaders in which she requires that one person just listen—no interruptions, not even affirmations, not a murmur, just listen (Reeves and Allison 2010). It seems so simple, yet after only a couple of minutes, most participants are visibly uncomfortable, and few of them make it through the four minutes of listening without some sort of interjection. The simple act of listening, it turns out, is not simple at all, and it requires exceptional levels of intentional focus. This requires discipline—including a visible timer—and the willingness to tolerate some silence rather than giving in to the impulse to fill any moments of silent contemplation with more talk.

. . . .

The simple act of listening, it turns out, is not simple at all, and it requires exceptional levels of intentional focus.

. . . .

Intense, focused, and uninterrupted listening is essential not only in teacher collaborative teams but also in the classroom. Students need to feel safe expressing themselves and, in particular, need to know that it is safe to make mistakes—one of the most essential elements of learning (Reeves 2021b). As we noted in Chapter 3, when students fear making mistakes because of the threat of humiliation for errors, all hopes for universal participation will be dashed on the shoals of fear. The same happens in adult learning environments when the impatient administrator or meeting leader asks, "Any questions?" with the implicit expectation that there are none, as the presenter has made everything so perfectly clear.

HOW COLLABORATION HELPS STUDENTS

The late Robert Slavin, of Johns Hopkins University and a giant in educational research, amassed decades of evidence to support the impact of effective collaboration for student learning (Slavin 2011). Effective collaboration can have a positive impact on student academic achievement, often as a result of the rich feedback students receive from their peers, but it can also improve their social abilities and emotional connections with other students (Burns 2016). Despite the promises of student collaboration, every teacher has witnessed well-intended collaborative exercises fall apart, typically as a result of one student doing the work while others are simply along for the ride.

Peer feedback can be a powerful support for improved achievement, but only if the feedback is accurate, specific, and timely. While we have noticed teachers require that peer feedback must be positive—"If you can't say anything nice, then don't say anything at all"—this limit violates the principle of *accuracy* that is vital for effective feedback. Moreover, when Annamaria says, "I know that James made a mistake in his essay, but I didn't want to tell him because it might hurt his feelings," then not only does James not benefit from feedback that would have made him a better writer, but Annamaria is denied the opportunity to learn how to give constructive feedback in a kind and thoughtful manner.

To make collaborative experiences in the classroom effective for student learning, then 100% engagement must be the norm for every group. This means that every student has a specific role to play in the group, and that students know that they add value to the group not merely by doing their individual tasks but by attentively reviewing and commenting on the tasks of their peers. We explicitly reject the typical task orientation that is labeled collaborative learning but is in fact anti-collaborative. Kennedy will draw the pictures, Blake will give the oral presentation, Wilson will write the report, and Taylor will do the graphs. While that division of labor is better than the typical situation in which one student performs all tasks (perhaps because that student was burned on a previous group project that did not go well), we insist that effective collaboration requires full engagement by all students with the expectation that they all contribute to the success of the group—not just the success of one piece of the work.

We understand the social dynamics of the classroom, and that is why students who are not used to looking at and providing feedback on a piece of work—perhaps an essay, a map, or a lab report—should first practice with anonymous work where no one knows the identity of the author. The group's only responsibility is to help those anonymous authors improve their work. After some practice with anonymous work, they can more confidently begin the work required to review and support the work of their friends and classmates.

. . . .

We continue to find many rubrics ambiguous and reliant on academic language beyond the grade level of the students who should be using them.

. . . .

In addition to the requirement for accuracy, students in collaborative teams must be *specific and timely* in how they provide feedback to support the best possible work. Although scoring rubrics have been around for decades, we continue to find many of them—including those from publishers and associated with state tests—ambiguous, reliant on academic language beyond the grade level of the students who should be using them, and generally unhelpful. Just as some of the best practices in engagement in Chapter 2 often take place in elementary grades and need to be expanded and applied at secondary and post-secondary classrooms, the same is true with respect to the specificity of feedback that students need. There is no Goldilocks "just right" scoring rubric, so we are left with guidance that is either too ambiguous or too specific, and when communicating academic expectations to students, the latter approach is almost always better. As with many readers, we have listened to students explain the rules of a game on the playground, and they are marvelously specific. "You can go *here*, but you can't go *there*. You can do *this*, but you can't do *that*." There are more than a few secondary, undergraduate, and graduate students who would benefit from that sort of specificity. One of the great misunderstandings about nurturing student creativity and intellectual growth is that constraints are the enemy of creativity. The evidence is to the contrary (Reeves and Reeves 2016). As Howard Gardner, one of the greatest advocates for student creativity, said, you can't think outside the box until you first understand the box (Gardner 2010).

· ·

One of the great misunderstandings about nurturing student creativity and intellectual growth is that constraints are the enemy of creativity.

· ·

The collaborative team meeting was not going well. The principal, Ms. Connor, insisted that each team should look at a piece of student work and evaluate it. How hard could that be? Principal Connor was about to find out. Collaborative scoring conferences were a bloodbath of conflicting opinions.

"That may be your standards," said Mr. Hazel, "but they are not my standards."

"Wait," the principal interrupted. "We all have the same standards and this is the same scoring rubric. How can we be so different?"

Mr. Hazel was prepared for the argument. "Look," he said. "The rubric says that proficient is 'mostly error free' and this essay clearly has a lot of errors. It's not proficient, and I'm not going to give this student credit for it."

"Are you kidding me?" Ms. Gunzelman asked. "This is a great essay, with a clear topic sentence, transitions, and conclusions. Sure, there were some spelling and grammar mistakes, but it clearly meets our standards."

The argument continued until Ms. Connor called for a timeout and said the words that guided every impasse she had experienced in faculty disagreements. "The enemy is not each other," she reminded them. "The enemy is ambiguity. Let's fix this scoring rubric until we can all agree on what proficient student work looks like. If we can't do that, students will never know what we expect of them."

LEADING FOR COLLABORATION AND ENGAGEMENT

Just as skillful classroom teachers respond to minute-to-minute changes in the classroom, noticing who is perplexed, who is bored, and who is five seconds away from a meltdown, so also must school leaders be adaptive to the professional learning environment around them. One central question leaders should consider after the years of the global pandemic and the pervasive impact it has had on students and teachers is this: How are things different? How is your schedule today different from 2019? How is the conduct of your staff meetings and teacher team meetings different? How have your leadership—policies, practices, and philosophies—changed? In too many cases, we find that the answer is, "not much." Not only have these parts of the school day been impervious to change, but desks remain in rows and columns, much as they were a century ago. Even when school funds have been invested in new furniture with the opportunity for more creative configurations, our observations of classrooms around the nation reveal that changes in furniture without changes in engagement practices yield nothing.

Leaders can and must take responsibility for modeling engagement strategies in the meetings they lead, and then expecting to see evidence of engagement in the classroom.

Brief ten- to fifteen-minute observations can yield a treasure trove of information about student engagement. There are wonderful models all around us—the music teacher who provides clear and specific feedback every few minutes, and the observer can hear how that feedback leads to better student performance. The kindergarten teacher who provides feedback and encouragement with every breath. The athletic coach who, unburdened by a red pen, gives feedback within seconds to players on how they can improve. Yet there are classes in which, despite expectations for engagement, ten or fifteen minutes can pass without a single interaction from a student. This was particularly problematic during virtual instruction, when synchronous learning was the time for teachers to deliver the curriculum, and asynchronous learning was the time for the student to practice. After nearly two years of that experiment, we have found very few cases where such a design worked any better than when teachers speak, demonstrate, instruct, and lecture without a hint of student engagement. We know school leaders are busy, but it does not require a full class period or a formally bargained-for meeting to just be in a classroom for ten minutes and determine the degree of engagement. If leaders will not do this, they are abdicating their responsibilities and cannot expect a culture of engagement to thrive.

. . . .

Leaders can and must take responsibility for modeling engagement strategies in the meetings they lead, and then expecting to see evidence of engagement in the classroom.

. . . .

Leaders can also model and observe effective checks for understanding. Phrases like "everybody with me?" and "any questions?" must give way to meaningful dialogue. "Claude, I see that you and Katrina disagree on this answer. Please help me understand how you reached your conclusion?" "Andrew, I know that you liked the story that we read, and I'm really interested to learn more about why you liked it." At more advanced levels, more meaningful checks for understanding might sound like this: "I really like the precise way in which you recorded your data from the experiment and how you drew a conclusion from that data. But tell me, how might another scientist, looking at the same data, draw a different conclusion?"

. . . .

Leaders must notice, appreciate, encourage, and replicate best practices at every turn.

. . . .

Finally, leaders must notice, appreciate, encourage, and replicate best practices at every turn. Many new teachers joining our profession will learn everything they know about engagement from their fellow teachers and administrators. It is therefore essential that leaders systematically capture and share great practices. Some principals take short videos of teachers in action and interview students, catching their genuine excitement about what engagement means to them. One of the best practices we have seen for replicating best practices is colloquially known as the "science fair for adults," in which teachers use simple three-panel displays to show a specific challenge, a practice they used to address that challenge, and the student results—achievement, attendance, behavior, and engagement. We have seen teachers make significant transformations in their level of classroom engagement when, for example, a high school math teacher stopped expecting the students to answer the odd-numbered problems at home under the illusion that students were practicing the concepts learned in class and started having them work on all four walls of the classroom doing the practice right then—in front of the teacher—with immediate feedback from peers and the teacher. It is no surprise that when practice happens in this environment rather than the artificial environment of homework, students are more engaged, and the practice actually leads to better performance.

WHAT TEACHERS AND LEADERS CAN DO NOW

1. Model in every staff gathering effective engagement practices, such as universal participation and think time.

2. Conduct mini-observations of ten to fifteen minutes and, when possible, include a fellow classroom teacher. It is not necessary to have a long checklist or electronic devices to record the observer's notes. The sole look-for is effective student engagement, and the teacher who is being observed deserves the courtesy of immediate and specific feedback on exactly what the observers saw and did not see.

3. Devote time in a staff meeting to critically review and reconstruct a scoring rubric for each grade level so that teachers leave with something that they can use immediately to provide more effective feedback to students. Remember, specificity beats ambiguity every time.

4. Invite a cordial debate on a topic of common interest where reasonable people can have different points of view. For example, when encouraging student creativity, to what degree should we have constraints on their work? What are effective economic and noneconomic ways to recognize and reward great professional performance? Divergent thinking in a psychologically safe environment leads to more authentic discussions and better leadership decision making.

5. Convert the next planned staff meeting to a "work only" session on teaching priorities. No announcements, no sharing of the latest information from higher headquarters. Just work, and thereby scream respect for teacher time.

CHAPTER SIX

Leading for Engagement

iStock.com/SDI Productions

In this chapter, you will learn about . . .

- Leadership at every level: from the classroom to the boardroom
- Challenging the leadership-management dichotomy
- How leaders support—and undermine—engagement
- The hallmarks of an engaged staff
- Engaging communities

In the final chapter of this book, we consider the vital role of leadership for engagement. The first five chapters dealt with the five Cs of engagement: connections, commitments, collaboration, challenge, and control. The glue that holds the five Cs together is leadership.

We cast a wide net, considering not only student engagement but the engagement of staff members and communities. The literature on leadership is vast, and much of it is unburdened by systematic research. Too many consumers of leadership books prefer anecdotes to evidence, often due to the association of an event—business success, international terrorism, wars, and so on—with the person who was in a position of leadership. This genre of leadership literature illogically associates the latter with the former. Jack Welch (Welch 2003) was lionized as the greatest business leader of the 20th century, even though his forced ranking system for employee evaluation was subsequently discredited and abandoned and his "from the gut" decisions proved disastrous for shareholders and the executives unlucky enough to inherit Welch's decisions. After Welch departed GE with a severance package of almost half a billion dollars, the company he led with apparent success began to fail, with the stock price plummeting, employees laid off, wages stagnant, and CEO pay continuing to soar (Gelles 2022). Self-aggrandizement, it seems, may sell books, but it is not linked to sustainable results.

Engagement does not occur in a vacuum, but rather in an environment in which leaders consistently nurture and encourage the practices that lead to engagement. This requires time and attention, both among the rarest treasures of busy leaders. Time is required because engagement at the classroom level requires consistent classroom observations and a high tolerance for mistakes. The attention of leaders is fragmented among many competing demands, from parents to discipline to curriculum to data analysis to an endless series of meetings and requirements from the district office. There is apparently little perceived irony in the requirement that principals attend mandatory district meetings about the importance of being present in classrooms.

. . . .

We contend that you cannot be a great leader without also being an effective manager of time, people, and projects.

. . . .

In this chapter, we consider how leaders can support—or undermine—engagement. We begin with our understanding of the essentials of leadership at every level, including teacher-leaders, principals, superintendents, and policy makers. We enter controversial ground when we challenge the pervasive leadership-management dichotomy, a staple of university graduate classes in leadership. This is the belief that leaders think grand visions and managers are just the hapless schleps who create a safe and secure learning environment, align curriculum and assessment, attend to the daily needs of students and faculty, and make the school and district run. We contend that you cannot be a great leader without also being an effective manager of time, people, and projects. Next, we consider how leaders have inadvertently undermined engagement with the ambiguous expectations surrounding classroom walkthroughs, learning walks, classroom observations, and both formal and informal evaluation systems. The chapter concludes with a consideration of staff and community engagement— central obligations of school and district leadership.

LEADERSHIP AT EVERY LEVEL: FROM THE CLASSROOM TO THE BOARDROOM

Although leadership is often associated with a title with positional authority, our observation is that the most effective leaders exert moral authority. People follow them not because they are required to follow orders, but because they are deeply invested in the success of their schools and the students they serve. Moreover, they follow the leader because of the trust and credibility that the leader has earned (Kouzes 2011). Leaders will be forgiven for many mistakes if they have established credibility, but without this essential asset, their prowess in data analysis, strategic planning, and communication will be useless. This is why classroom educators and administrators can, early in their careers, demonstrate greater influence than their colleagues with greater experience and more advanced degrees who have not established credibility or who have squandered it through habits of exaggerated claims and assertions unsupported by evidence. Credible leaders quickly admit their mistakes and help the entire organization learn from them, while other leaders fear acknowledgment of error, as it may be a sign of weakness.

. . . .

Leaders will be forgiven for many mistakes if they have established credibility.

. . . .

Teacher-leaders willingly share their classroom data, assessments, and student work with colleagues, knowing that this sharing and the vulnerability that accompanies it is at the heart of effective professional collaboration (DuFour and Fullan 2013). This is in sharp contrast to the more common phenomenon in which teachers are happy to collaborate on lesson plans and presentations but draw the line at revealing data on their students or sharing samples of student work. Whatever the label of their team meetings, often referred to in the parlance of professional learning communities (PLCs), the reality is that without the sort of teacher leadership we are describing—comprehensive sharing of student data and student work and the professional vulnerability that goes with it—they are engaged in nothing more than PLC Lite (DuFour and Reeves 2016).

CHALLENGING THE LEADERSHIP-MANAGEMENT DICHOTOMY

"But what do we do right now?" The question punctured the enthusiasm in the room after a two-day leadership retreat. The district team had, after much struggle, come to a consensus on values, mission, and vision. They knew that their role was not merely to be managers of the schools and the district that they served, but to be leaders. Nevertheless, the question hung in the air: "What do we do now?" The 24 leaders of the district leadership team had worked long into the night to craft a three-paragraph vision statement. They ensured that every voice was represented in the mission statement. They were crystal clear on their values. But when faced with the question "But what do we do right now?", they were stuck.

Since the seminal *Harvard Business Review* article, "Leaders and Managers: Are They Different?" (Zaleznik 1992), people in organizations and most university leadership classes have been careful to distinguish their roles. Managers, after all, are the second-rate leader wannabes, while leaders, by contrast, think great thoughts and produce grand visions. Among the many bilious statements about managers and leaders is that leaders do the right things, while managers merely do things right. The late Warren Bennis, who popularized this distinction, also contended:

- "The manager relies on control; the leader inspires trust."

- "The manager is a copy; the leader is an original."

- "The manager accepts the status quo; the leader challenges it." (Boynton 2016)

· ·

The essence of managing people is feedback and communication.

· ·

While Bennis, whose experiences as a university president, leadership scholar, and global leadership guru, was right in many things, his emphasis on the leadership-management dichotomy was wrong. In the 21st century, it is not possible to be a great leader without also mastering fundamental management skills. These include managing time, projects, people, money, and technology. Moreover, managers who attend to the details of these areas must also not merely "do things right." They must, as leaders do, challenge the status quo, inspire trust, and bring innovation and creativity to their jobs every day. In an environment in which technology can be overwhelming, leaders must have the discipline—the management discipline—to focus their time and energy and the resources of the organizations that they lead on what matters most. Unfortunately, the vast majority of leaders do not lead professional lives of focus but are fragmented into disconnected priorities that lead to organizational confusion and ambiguity (Newport 2021).

Because good leaders are effective managers of their time, they give themselves and the stakeholders they serve the gift of uninterrupted time for deep work—focused attention and intellectual energy without e-mails, texts, calls, social media, or any other diversion that is short of a life-threatening emergency. We counsel leaders to start with just two 45-minute periods per week at an out-of-office location—perhaps the library or other room that gives them the rare gift of uninterrupted time and focus. We are not naïve and realize that the daily lives of educational leaders and teachers are full of interruptions. That is why we receive so many e-mails and texts late in the evening when leaders should be with their families or getting much-needed rest, but find that these are the only hours available for intellectual work that is necessary to achieve their goals.

. . . .

Managing people is not about the Byzantine complexity of most evaluation systems, but rather about simple and clear expectations.

. . . .

The essentials of time management are simple but neither simplistic nor easy. These include a daily prioritized task list, which is just what it means. It is updated daily to reflect the priorities of that day. It is prioritized so that each task is done in sequence—yesterday's item 6 may be today's number 1. The items are tasks—not projects. In general, tasks are activities that can be completed in a single setting—usually 45 or fewer minutes. For busy school leaders for whom 45 minutes may seem an eternity, it may be more appropriate to define tasks as an activity requiring no more than 15 minutes. Everything else is a project, and projects must then be divided into tasks—increments of no more than those 15-minute activities. By "list," we mean a clearly visible list. Some leaders prefer automated systems, such as Trello, which can be sorted every day based on priority. Other leaders have their list on a whiteboard so that every staff member can see precisely where the leader is on the list and can be assured that their favored task has not been neglected.

The essence of managing people is feedback and communication. One of the most common management mistakes that we observe is the limiting of feedback to colleagues to evaluations, often done toward the end of the year. Evaluation is an inherently adversarial process in which the leader is the judge and the subordinate is the defendant in the dock. Feedback, by contrast, is a reciprocal process in which the leader can share objective observations about the most recent classroom walkthrough, team meeting, cabinet meeting, or other activity. Managing people is not about the Byzantine complexity of most evaluation systems, but rather about simple and clear expectations. For example:

When I last visited your classroom, I noticed that you called on Maria three times in a row, as she was the only student with her hand in the air. That allowed the other 34 students to be completely disengaged. When I come back next week, I'd like to see you experiment with equity sticks or other random calling systems, so that every student has an equal probability of being engaged in the lesson. If you need help on how to use equity sticks effectively, I'd be happy to take your class for 30 minutes while you observe Ms. Martinez, who has had great results with this technique.

When I watched your collaborative team meeting, I really appreciated how thoughtful you were in getting everyone to participate. The shared lesson plans were very effective, and it was clear that people appreciate that. What I didn't see was student data and examples of real student work. When I observe your team next week, I'd like to see a greater emphasis on student data, organized by classroom, and some collaborative scoring of student work.

When I watched the last cabinet meeting, I noticed that the presentations from the facilities and finance departments were one-way information flows—you really didn't need a meeting for those presentations. At the next cabinet meeting, would you consider asking people to distribute the information before the meeting and focus the cabinet time only on deliberation and inquiry about the presentations rather than just passive listening?

HOW LEADERS SUPPORT—AND UNDERMINE—ENGAGEMENT

While nearly everyone approves of the idea of student engagement, there is a significant disconnect between what leaders expect in terms of engagement and what teachers hear from leaders. While leaders may expect engagement to be a highly interactive discussion, with students volunteering to make an effort in tackling a difficult question, making mistakes, getting feedback, and then improving their understanding, what teachers sometimes strive for is the "perfect" classroom, in which students diligently answer every question, there are no mistakes, and the room is quiet with the exceptions of presentations by the teacher and selected students. This is the illusion of engagement (Gupta and Reeves 2021). It is therefore essential that leaders make their expectations clear about what engagement really means:

I'm not looking for the perfect classroom in which you call only on students who know the answers. That's not learning. I'm looking for real-time teaching and learning. That means that you call—I hope randomly—on students and when they don't know the answer, I have the opportunity to see great teaching and learning take place. I'm also looking for meaningful checks for understanding. Even when a student has provided a correct answer, I'm asking you to probe more deeply and help the entire class learn the reasoning and logic behind the answer— not just the answer itself.

Although this learning environment describes the classroom that most leaders would like to see, many teachers perceive an unstated preference for good order and discipline and obedient students who have the right answer to every question, followed by affirmation from the teacher. The silence and apparently good behavior of students whose eyes follow the teacher in these classrooms can earn praise from many administrators, sending the message that risk taking, including wrong answers and the noise associated with actively engaged small groups, is not appreciated.

. . . .

The enemy of engagement is the abrupt "Any questions?"

. . . .

If leaders expect to see genuine engagement in the classroom, then they need to model this expectation in staff meetings. The enemy of engagement is the abrupt "Any questions?" with the body language of the interrogator clearly signaling that there had better not be any questions. Staff meetings and professional learning seminars must model the engagement that we seek from students, and that implies the elements of great teaching and learning for any age:

- Pre-assessment

- Interesting and dynamic scenarios that make it clear that this information is worth learning

- Affirmation of mistakes

- Persistent checks for understanding

- A fearless approach to every challenge

THE HALLMARKS OF AN ENGAGED STAFF

While student engagement is the focus of this book, we have learned that students take their cues from the adults in the building. It's not possible to have highly engaged students when the staff is clearly in an environment of fear and distrust. When the staff displays a fear of making mistakes, then don't expect the students to be enthusiastic about taking risks and making the mistakes that inevitably accompany risk, innovation, and creativity.

. . . .

When the staff displays a fear of making mistakes, then don't expect the students to be enthusiastic about taking risks.

. . . .

In order to assess the degree of staff engagement, it is helpful to consider both formal and informal staff interaction. Formal interactions, such as staff meetings, team meetings, and other scheduled opportunities for staff interaction, typically take one of two directions. The first is most common—the leader talking 90% of the time with the participants (an audience, really) listening to the announcements and pronouncements from the person directing the meeting. These are the meetings that give rise to the coffee mug emblazoned with the statement, "Another meeting that could have been an e-mail." Let's call this the leader-focused meeting. The second type of meeting has as its focus deliberation and inquiry. In these meetings, there are no announcements or presentations. Participants are expected to have read preparatory materials in advance. Agenda items end not with periods but with question marks so that it is clear that every person attending is expected to engage in solving challenging problems that are important to everyone. Let's call this the inquiry-focused meeting.

The Leader-Focused Meeting

In the leader-focused meeting, consensus is vital, and divergent views are shunned. Questions such as, "What evidence do you have for this claim and recommendation?" are met with a wounded reply of, "Don't you trust me?" rather than a coherent production of essential evidence. To the extent that there were divergent points of view, those disagreements were buried before the meeting was convened, so that the leader has the illusion of unanimity and can confidently say to senior leaders and policy makers, "My entire team is on board with this recommendation." Despite the overwhelming evidence that divergent thinking leads to better decision making (Paige and Amrein 2020), many leaders prefer consensus today rather than a realistic consideration of the fact that every decision has both advantages and disadvantages, rewards and risks, that should be explored fully before a final decision is made. This is particularly true when one person has a disproportionate amount of information—technology, finance, law—and other leaders tend to defer to the expertise of the few.

· ·

Despite the overwhelming evidence that divergent thinking leads to better decision making (Paige and Amrein 2020), many leaders prefer consensus.

· ·

The Inquiry-Focused Meeting

In contrast to the leader-focused meeting is the inquiry-focused meeting in which questions are not only welcome but required. Rather than taking up all the available oxygen in the room, the leader in the inquiry-focused meeting will persistently ask members, "What else do you need to know in order to either support or oppose this proposal?" When participants meet this challenge with stony silence, that is a clear signal that their primary purpose in the meeting is claiming a space—a seat at the table and the perceived prestige that goes along with it. This is why many meetings of senior leadership teams with twenty or more people are an egregious waste of time. The science of effective meetings is clear that when the number of participants exceeds seven people (Rogelberg 2019), it is a prescription for a colossal waste of time. One way we have seen senior leaders make better use of meetings at the cabinet level is to have participants in the meeting only for the agenda items to which they make a relevant contribution (Reeves 2020b).

Whether the meeting is a team of third-grade teachers or the cabinet meeting of the most senior leaders of the district, the contrast between the leader-focused meeting and inquiry-focused meeting is the same. Just look at the ratio of leader talk to the contributions of participants. Observe who says nothing and who engages in grandstanding, making speeches that are not relevant to the topic at hand. If a leader expects a high degree of student engagement, with teachers talking less and listening more, then the leader must model that expectation in the interactions with staff members.

Beyond the formal interactions among staff members, such as meetings, informal communications can also be very revealing about the degree of engagement among the staff. The same spirit of inquiry, which is the hallmark of effective formal interactions, is also evident when there is a culture of collaboration in a school or central office. One hears questions such as, "I saw your students' writing in the hallway and it was really impressive! Please tell me more about what you did to accomplish that." "The data you presented at the last board meeting was so clear and understandable. Could you help me learn more about how you translated data in a way that was so easy to understand?" These informal hallway interactions represent the real culture of an organization, a culture in which questions and requests for learning are not signs of weakness, but symptoms of individual and organizational learning.

ENGAGING COMMUNITIES

The power of community engagement has been documented extensively by Georgetown management professor Christine Porath, whose research in successful community organizations, ranging from health care to education to support for homeless people, has a common thread. Although people yearn for interpersonal connections and a sense of belonging, traditional sources of community have languished (Porath 2022). Vibrant communities are strongly linked to higher levels of engagement, and higher levels of engagement are linked to personal happiness as well as economic stability. Porath uses the *Bantu* word often cited by South African Archbishop Desmond Tutu, *Ubuntu*. It is the essence of being human. The term means that we cannot exist in isolation but are fundamentally interconnected with others. The philosophy of *Ubuntu* is associated with generosity, kindness, and modesty. Our individual accomplishments are a result of who we are as a group and not merely individual distinction. It implies mutual respect, a commitment to helping one another, and connections among individuals and groups.

. . . .

The philosophy of *Ubuntu* is associated with generosity, kindness, and modesty.

. . . .

Although the focus of this book has been on education, the support that schools need in the post-pandemic world cannot be limited to student performance alone. Amazing examples of *Ubuntu* in the educational world occurred when schools were just starting to re-open, but many students remained at home. In communities as diverse as Pueblo, Colorado; Newark, New Jersey; and Greenfield, Wisconsin, teachers and administrators scoured laundry mats, thrift stores, playgrounds, and community gathering places to find students who needed to be in school and, as the first priority, reconnect with families who had grown distrustful of government institutions in general and schools in particular. They did not threaten parents with sanctions or send truant officers to remind families of the legal consequences of failing to attend school. Rather, they relied on building communities through shared trust, respect, and engagement. It should not take another pandemic for schools and districts to learn the value of community engagement. We have heard the cynical observations of parents and community leaders who note that the only time educators and leaders really get into the community is when there is a bond issue to be passed or a contested school board election is on the calendar. Authentic engagement with our communities occurs not because of what we all need from them materially or politically, but what we need from one another emotionally and psychologically.

Porath's research concludes that engagement is not merely with other people, but with ourselves. Our mission as educators and leaders can dominate our lives, and we are fortunate indeed to have jobs that provide a sense of purpose and meaning. However, when someone asks how we are doing, and the initial response is about how things are going at school, then it is possible, Porath suggests, that our priorities are out of order. In order to be fully present at school, we must also be fully present for friends and family and the community connections that are vital to finding joy.

Another key to community engagement is making real, not merely virtual, connections. Facebook has the technology to allow friends to know if they are geographically close. "Hey—we're just a few blocks apart from one another—let's have coffee!" But Facebook does not have such a feature. Why? Because the social media giants that control so much of our information, advertising, and expenditures of time and money are not profitable when we are talking face to face with friends. These companies thrive on the illusion of friendship because they are only transforming eyeballs into profits when we are staring at screens (Hari 2022). Real engagement is not a mass e-mail, a social media post, a tweet, or a picture on Instagram. While Archbishop Tutu was certainly a master of the mass communication technology of his day, his influence came from the personal connections that he modeled and fostered around the diverse peoples and languages in the nation he helped to create.

. . . .

Real engagement is not a mass e-mail, a social media post, a tweet, or a picture on Instagram.

. . . .

In this chapter, we have explored how leaders at every level, from the classroom to the boardroom, foster engagement. While a compelling leadership vision is important for every school and district, vision alone is insufficient. The much-maligned but absolutely essential management skills of how we use time, engage with people, and coordinate projects give us the tools that are necessary to make leadership visions a reality. While we do not believe that leaders intentionally undermine engagement, examples abound of implicit messages from leaders that convey an expectation of an error-free environment. This leads to a climate of fear among students and staff members, which is the antithesis of effective engagement. Just as an engaged classroom is characterized by joyful and fearless student interactions, an engaged staff is reflected in their ability to have conversations, debates, and deep inquiry, without fear of retribution. Leaders who foster this sort of engagement are not threatened by questions or suggestions that there are better ways to achieve educational objectives. Finally, we made the case for engaging communities on a deep interpersonal level. If you found the ideas in this book of value, we hope that you will share some of these ideas with colleagues, students, parents, and friends. We need engagement now more than ever, and we hope that you have found some tools to further engagement in the roles that you play in school and in your community.

Appendix

Active Participation Techniques
to **SUPERCHARGE** Your Lessons

ORAL RESPONSES

TECHNIQUE	IMPLEMENTATION STEPS
Choral Response	1. Ask a question. 2. Provide students with think time (3 to 5 seconds). 3. State verbal cue (i.e., "Sound?" "Answer?" "Everyone?") followed by the physical signal (lowered hand, tap, finger snap, etc.) to prompt students to answer together. 4. Provide constructive feedback as needed.
Think–Pair–Share	1. Assign partners. 2. Designate partner roles (i.e., A–B partners, 1–2 partners, peanut butter–jelly partners). 3. **Think:** Ask a question and provide think time (3 to 5 seconds). 4. **Pair:** Direct students to discuss their answers with a partner (designate who shares—As share first, then Bs; Bs share, As summarize, etc.). 5. **Share:** Call on three to five students to share out to the whole class, *or*, if the answer is short and the wording is the same, do a choral response and have all students share at once.
Inside-Outside Circle	1. Divide students into two equal numbered groups. Designate one group as 1s and the other group as 2s. 2. Direct 1s to make a circle, facing out, and 2s to make a circle around the 1s, facing in. 3. Direct students to pair up; each student in the inside circle should face and partner up with one student from the outside circle. 4. Place a list of questions on the classroom whiteboard, interactive whiteboard, document camera, etc. for all students to see. 5. Direct 1s to ask questions and 2s to answer. Partners then switch roles and 2s ask questions and 1s answer. 6. Give a signal for movement. For example, ask students in the outer circle to rotate two steps to the left. 7. Repeat the questioning process and movement within the circle until all questions are answered.

(Continued)

(Continued)

TECHNIQUE	IMPLEMENTATION STEPS
Numbered Heads	1. Number off students from 1 to 4. This is their numbered head team.
	2. Ask a question or give a problem and provide think time.
	3. Direct students to lean forward (put heads together) to discuss the answer with their team. They must ensure that everyone on the team knows the answer.
	4. Randomly call out a number from 1 to 4 (use a spinner, toss a die, draw popsicle sticks, etc.).
	5. On each team, the student whose number was called stands to verbally share the answer.
	6. Once the signal is given, the designated students share their answers.
	7. Repeat with additional questions. Give team points for correct responses if desired.
Study-Tell-Help-Check	1. Assign partners.
	2. **Study:** Give students a short time to individually study their notes, handouts, textbooks, etc. (1 to 2 minutes).
	3. **Tell:** Direct students to tell their partner all they remember about the topic without consulting their reference materials.
	4. **Help:** Direct partners to help out by asking their partner questions, giving hints, or filling in any missing information.
	5. **Check:** When both partners feel they have shared all of their information, have them go back to their reference materials to check their responses and locate any information they might have missed.
Sentence Starters	Prompt discussion about a topic among the group by using sentence starters. This can be embedded within choral responses, paired responses, or small group responses.
	• I agree/disagree because . . .
	• I'm still confused about . . .
	• I understand why you'd say that, but . . .
	• And then there was another example of that . . .
	• I understand and would like to add . . .
	• There is another piece of evidence that . . .
	• Another way you might interpret that is . . .

TECHNIQUE	IMPLEMENTATION STEPS
Follow On	1. Ask a question. 2. Provide think time (3 to 5 seconds). 3. Call on a student to share their answer with the class. Then prompt students to "follow on" the previous answer through the use of prompts such as "Add on . . ." or "Develop . . ." or "Evidence?" **Example:** **Teacher:** What bad news in this chapter does Wilbur get from the old sheep? (Teacher provides think time, then calls on a student.) **John:** Wilbur finds out that he is going to be killed. **Teacher:** *Excellent*, John. *Add on*, Mary. **Mary:** Wilbur finds out he is going to be killed at Christmastime. **Teacher:** You're right, Mary. Now, work with your partner to find *text evidence* for Mary's answer. (Teacher gives partners 15 to 20 seconds to find evidence, then calls on a student.) **Teacher:** *Evidence*, Marcus. **Marcus:** On page 49, it says, "There's a regular conspiracy around here to kill you at Christmastime. Everybody is in the plot—Lurvey, Zuckerman, even John Arable." **Teacher:** Very good! Now, work with your partner to *develop* and discuss an interesting word in the text that Marcus just read—*conspiracy*. What does that mean? What clues from the text help you to figure that out?
Pause and Connect	1. **Pause:** After 10 to 15 minutes of lecture or learning of new information, ask students to *pause*. 2. **Connect:** Students should then reflect with a partner or small group by using one or more of the following connections: • *Summarize:* What have you learned so far? • *Question:* Students answer a focus question related to the content presented. • *Highlight:* What do you want to be sure to remember? (Students can highlight in their notes.) • *Experience:* What personal experiences have you had that connect with the content? • *Predict:* What do you predict will be covered next?

(Continued)

(Continued)

TECHNIQUE	IMPLEMENTATION STEPS
Whip Around	1. Ask a question (use the type of question that can have many possible answers) and provide think time (3 to 5 seconds). 2. Whip around the room (up and down rows, counterclockwise around the room, etc.) as students quickly say their answers with no intervening comments by the teacher or other students.
Talking Chips	1. Place students in groups of three to four. 2. Pass out two to three "talking chips" to each student (items such as counting chips, buttons, paper squares, etc.). 3. Ask discussion questions. Have students then discuss. As students contribute to the discussion, they place a talking chip in the center of the table. 4. Group discussion continues until each student in the group has used all of their chips. When a student has used up all of their chips, they no longer talk. Meanwhile, you monitor group discussions and take notes. 5. Signal to bring the group back together and then share notes and/or call on two to three students to share out key points from the group discussion.
Four Corners	1. Label each corner of the room with a content-relevant number, name, word, or phrase (Strongly Agree, Agree, Disagree, Strongly Disagree; Multiple Choice—A, B, C, D; four key characters from the text, etc.). 2. Pass out an index card to each student. Ask a question and have students individually write down the corner they would like to choose. They should then turn over their card without talking. 3. Say "Four Corners!," which signals students to move to their chosen corner. 4. At the corner, have students find a partner and discuss their answers and their rationale for choosing them. **Examples:** • Which character from the text is the most stubborn? Be ready to cite text evidence to back up your answer. • Choose one of the posted four words and use it in two sentences that are at least eight words long each. • Do you strongly agree, agree, disagree, or strongly disagree with the following statement? *Frankenstein was a novel where the monsters behaved humanely and the humans behaved like monsters.* Be ready to cite text evidence to back up your answer. • Do you strongly agree, agree, disagree, or strongly disagree with the following statement? *In Chapter 4 of A Separate Peace, Gene is responsible for Ginny's fall.* Be ready to cite text evidence to back up your answer.

WRITTEN RESPONSES

TECHNIQUE	IMPLEMENTATION STEPS
Think-Write-Pair-Share	1. Assign partners and designate partner roles (i.e., A–B partners,1–2 partners, peanut butter–jelly partners). 2. **Think:** Ask a question and provide think time (3 to 5 seconds). 3. **Write:** Direct students to write their answers. While students are writing, use a clipboard and paper to record students' ideas as you walk around and monitor responses. 4. **Pair:** Direct students to what they've written with a partner (designate who shares first—i.e., As share, then Bs). If their partner shares something they didn't have, they may add it to their answer. 5. **Share:** Place a clipboard with notes under a document camera and share out with the whole class.
Think-Write-Show	1. **Think:** Ask a question and provide think time. 2. **Write:** Direct students to write their answers. 3. **Show:** Direct students to hold up their board and show what they've written. This is a great opportunity for the teacher to formatively assess, provide feedback, and adjust instruction as necessary.
QuickWrite/QuickDraw	1. Ask a question or give a prompt. 2. Direct students to write or draw answers (short timeframe). 3. Give a signal to finish, like "Finish your sentence/picture. Put down your pencil and look up when you're done." 4. Have students share work—individually, in partners, or in small groups.
Roundtable	1. Place students in groups of four. 2. Ask a question or give a topic/problem. 3. Direct students to simultaneously respond to the question by writing or drawing (or using manipulatives). 4. Provide a signal for when the time is up. 5. Direct student to pass their papers one person clockwise. 6. Have students then continue to add to what was already on the paper.

ACTION RESPONSES

TECHNIQUE	IMPLEMENTATION STEPS
Show Me	1. Establish with students the appropriate response signal (thumbs up, show the number of fingers, stand up, hands on head, etc.). 2. Ask a question and provide think time. 3. Say "Show Me"; have students respond. **Examples:** • Thumbs up if what I say is an example of the word *reluctant*; thumbs down if it is not. • Stand up if the word I say has the same beginning sound as *mat*. • Say and hold up a finger for each sound you hear in *cup*. • Hands on your head if these two words are synonyms. Touch your toes if they are antonyms. • Before you spell the word, tap each sound you hear on your desk.
Response Cards	1. Direct students to write possible responses in each corner of the index card (i.e., A-B-C-D) *or* on the front and back of the response card (Yes/No, Agree/Disagree, etc.) *or* use prepared response cards. 2. Ask a question or give a prompt. 3. Have students privately select a number/letter/word answer from the response card. 4. On your signal, students hold up the response card for you to see. 5. Monitor responses for student understanding of skill or strategy and provide feedback and reteaching as needed.
Act It Out!	1. Ask a question where the answer can be physically demonstrated. 2. Have students "act it out" either in partners or small groups. 3. Call on three to five students to share with the class. **Examples:** • Tell class, "One of our vocabulary words is *reluctant*. Show your partner what your face looks like when you're reluctant to do something." • Number students off into groups of three. Assign 1s a character, 2s a character, and 3s a character. Students act out pages of the text.

TECHNIQUE	IMPLEMENTATION STEPS
Touch/Point	The Touch/Point method is particularly useful for teachers of primary students. Students should "show" their work or thinking by touching or pointing. The request for touching/pointing should ring throughout the lesson. **Examples:** • Put your finger on the title of the book. • Touch the letter. • Put your finger on the word. • Point to the answer in the text for the following question: Why did Meg's book fall in the puddle? *Note:* A simple directive such as "put your finger on the answer" followed by "Now, check your partner" helps increase the number of students on task and in the right place (Archer and Hughes 2011).

Source: Side by Side Consulting (n.d.).

References

Amabile, Teresa, and Steven Kramer. 2011. "The Power of Small Wins." *Harvard Business Review* (May 2011):70–81.

Anderson, Jill. 2022. "Harvard EdCast: The COVID Catch-up Challenge." Retrieved June 14, 2022 (https://www.gse.harvard.edu/news/22/04/harvard-edcast-covid-catch-challenge).

Archer, Anita L., and Charles A. Hughes. 2011. *Explicit Instruction: Effective and Efficient Teaching.* New York: The Guilford Press.

Argarwal, Pooja, and Patrice M. Bain. 2019. *Powerful Teaching: Unleash the Science of Learning.* San Francisco, CA: Wiley.

Aronson, Elliot. 2002. "Building Empathy, Compassion, and Achievement in the Jigsaw Classroom." Pp. 209–25 in *Improving Academic Achievement: Impact of Psychological Factors on Education,* edited by J. Aronson. Boston, MA: Academic Press.

Barth, F. Diane. 2018. "7 Ways to Fight Debilitating Sham." Retrieved April 6, 2022 (https://www.psychologytoday.com/us/blog/the-couch/201803/7-ways-fight-debilitating-shame).

Beshears, John, and Francesca Gino. 2015. "Leaders as Decision Architects." *Harvard Business Review.* Retrieved February 15, 2021 (https://hbr.org/2015/05/leaders-as-decision-architects).

Boynton, Andy. 2016. "Nine Things That Separate the Leaders from the Managers." (https://www.forbes.com/sites/andyboynton/2016/03/31/want-to-be-a-leader-not-just-a-manager-do-these-nine-things/?sh=506a23ec51e0).

Burns, Mary. 2016. "5 Strategies to Deepen Student Collaboration." Retrieved February 27, 2022 (https://www.edutopia.org/article/5-strategies-deepen-student-collaboration-mary-burns).

Chang, Hedy N., David Osher, Mara Schanfield, Jane Sundius, and Lauren Bauer. 2019. "Using Chronic Absence Data to Improve Conditions for Learning." *Attendance Works and American Institutes for Research (AIR).* (https://www.attendanceworks.org/wp-content/uploads/2019/06/Attendance_Works_Using_Chronic_Absence__091619.pdf).

Chew, Stephen L., and William J. Cerbin. 2020. "The Cognitive Challenges of Effective Teaching." *Journal of Economic Education* 52(1):17–40.

Chickering, Arthur W., and Stephen C. Ehrmann. 1996. "Implementing the Seven Principles: Technology as Lever." *AAHE Bulletin* 49(2):3–6.

Civil Rights Data Collection. 2019. "Chronic Absenteeism in the Nation's Schools: A Hidden Educational Crisis." U.S. Department of Education. (https://www2.ed.gov/datastory/chronicabsentee ism.html).

Cole, Carrie. 2017. "20 Active Participation Techniques to Supercharge Your Lessons!" Side by Side Educational Consulting. (https://sidebysideconsulting.com/2017/10/01/20-active-partici pation-techniques-to-supercharge-your-lessons)

Daly, Alan, Nienke Moolenar, Liou Yi-Hwa, Melissa Tuytens, and Miguel del Fresno. 2015. "Why So Difficult? Exploring Negative Relationships Between Educational Leaders: The Role of Trust, Climate, and Efficacy." *Journal of Education* 12(1):1–38.

Davis, Marcia H., Martha Abele Mac Iver, Robert W. Balfanz, Marc L. Stein, and Joanna Hornig Fox. 2019. "Implementation of an Early Warning Indicator and Intervention System." *Preventing School Failure* 63(1):77–88.

Donohoo, Jenni, John Hattie, and Rachel Eells. 2018. "The Power of Collective Efficacy." *Educational Leadership* 75(6):40–44.

Donovan, M. Suzanne, and John D. Bransford, eds. 2005. *How Students Learn: History, Mathematics, and Science in the Classroom.* Washington, DC: The National Academies Press.

Duckworth, Angela, Christopher Peterson, C., Michael D. Matthews, M., and Dennis R. Kelly. 2007. "Grit: Perseverance and Passion for Long-Term Goals." *Journal of Personality and Social Psychology,* 92(6):1087–1101.

DuFour, Richard, and Douglas Reeves. 2016. "The Futility of PLC Lite." *Phi Delta Kappan* 97(6):69–71.

DuFour, Richard, and Michael Fullan. 2013. *Cultures Built to Last: Systemic PLCs at Work.* Bloomington, IN: Solution Tree Press.

Dweck, Carol. 2007. *Mindset: The New Psychology of Success.* New York: Random House.

Dyson, James. (2021). *Invention: A Life.* New York, NY: Simon & Schuster.

Edmondson, Amy C. 2018. *The Fearless Organization: Creating Psychological Safety in the Workplace for Learning, Innovation, and Growth.* Hoboken, NJ: Wiley.

Eklund, Katie, Matthew K. Burns, Kari Oyen, Sarah DeMarchena, and Elizabeth M. McCollom. 2020. "Addressing Chronic Absenteeism in Schools: A Meta-Analysis of Evidence-Based Interventions." *School Psychology Review* 51(1):95–111.

Evans, Karen. 2018. "Why Relationships Are the Secret to Healthy Aging." Retrieved February 21, 2022 (https://great ergood.berkeley.edu/article/item/why_relationships_are_the_secret_to_healthy_aging).

Faddis, Toni, Douglas Fisher, and Nancy Frey. 2022. *Collaboration Through Collective Efficacy Cycles: A Playbook for Ensure All Students and Teachers Succeed.* Thousand Oaks, CA: Corwin.

Fisher, Douglas, and Nancy Frey. 2021. "Why Do Students Disengage?" *Educational Leadership* 79(1):76–77.

Fisher, Douglas, Nancy Frey, John Almarode, and Karen T. Flories, K. 2019. *PLC+: Better Decisions and Greater Impact by Design.* Thousand Oaks, CA: Corwin.

Fisher, Douglas, Nancy Frey, John Hattie, and Karen T. Flories. 2019a. *Becoming an Assessment-Capable Visible Learner, Grades 3–5: Learner's Notebook.* Thousand Oaks, CA: Corwin.

Fisher, Douglas, Nancy Frey, John Hattie, and Karen T. Flories. 2019b. *Becoming an Assessment-Capable Visible Learner, Grades 3–5: Teacher's Guide.* Thousand Oaks, CA: Corwin.

Fisher, Douglas, Nancy Frey, John Hattie, and Karen T. Flories. 2019c. *Becoming an Assessment-Capable Visible Learner, Grades 6–12: Learner's Notebook.* Thousand Oaks, CA: Corwin.

Fisher, Douglas, Nancy Frey, John Hattie, and Karen T. Flories. 2019d. *Becoming an Assessment-Capable Visible Learner, Grades 6–12: Teacher's Guide.* Thousand Oaks, CA: Corwin.

Fisher, Douglas, Nancy Frey, Russell J. Quaglia, Dominique Smith, and Lisa L. Lande. 2018. *Engagement by Design: Creating Learning Environments Where Students Thrive.* Thousand Oaks, CA: Corwin.

Frey, Nancy, and Douglas Fisher. 2008. "The Underappreciated Role of Humiliation in Middle School." *Middle School Journal* 39(5):4–13.

Frey, Nancy, and Douglas Fisher. 2013. *Rigorous Reading: Five Access Points for Helping Students Comprehend Complex Texts, K–12.* Thousand Oaks, CA: Corwin.

Frey, Nancy, Douglas Fisher, and John Almarode. 2021. *How Tutoring Works: Six Steps to Grow Motivation and Accelerate Student Learning.* Thousand Oaks, CA: Corwin.

Frey, Nancy, John Hattie, and Douglas Fisher. 2018. *Developing Assessment-Capable Visible Learners, Grades K–12: Maximizing Skill, Will, and Thrill.* Thousand Oaks, CA: Corwin.

Gardner, Howard. 2010. "Five Minds for the Future." P. 375 in *21st Century Skills: Rethinking How Students Learn.* Bloomington, IN: Solution Tree Press.

Gelles, David. 2022. *The Man Who Broke Capitalism: How Jack Welch Gutted the Heartland and Crushed the Soul of Corporate America—and How to Undo His Legacy.* New York, NY: Simon & Schuster.

Gieras, Jenny. 2020. "A Powerful Strategy for Fostering Student Motivation." Retrieved April 6, 2022 (https://www.edutopia.org/article/powerful-strategy-fostering-student-motivation).

Graham, Ruth. 2015. "The Tired, Lonely Downside of Working Creatively." *The Boston Globe*, October 4, p. 3.

Gregorio Mora-Ruano, Julio, Jorge Heine, and Markus Gebhardt. 2019. "Does Teacher Collaboration Improve Student Achievement? Analysis of the German PISA 2012 Sample." Retrieved February 26, 2022 (https://www.frontiersin.org/articles/10.3389/feduc.2019.00085/full).

Gupta, Neil, and Douglas Reeves. 2021. "The Engagement Illusion." *Educational Leadership* 78(4):58–63.

Guskey, Tom. 2020. "Flip the Script on Change: Experience Shapes Teachers' Attitudes and Beliefs." *The Learning Professional* 41(2):18–22.

Hari, Johann. 2022. *Stolen Focus: Why You Can't Pay Attention—and How to Think Deeply Again.* New York: Crown Business.

Hattie, John. 2009. *Visible Learning: A Synthesis of Over 800 Meta-Analyses Relating to Achievement.* London: Routledge.

Hattie, John. 2013. *Visible Learning for Teachers: Maximizing Impact on Learning.* London: Taylor and Francis.

Hickey, Maud. 2001. "An Application of Amabile's Consensual Assessment Technique for Rating the Creativity of Children's Musical Compositions." *Journal of Research in Music Education* 49(3):234–44.

Kiml, Tara. 2022. "Tackling Teacher Shortages: What Can States and Districts Do?" Retrieved February 26, 2022 (https://learningpolicyinstitute.org/blog/teacher-shortage-what-can-states-and-districts-do).

Kouzes, James. 2011. *Credibility: How Leaders Gain and Lose It, Why People Demand It.* 2nd ed. San Francisco, CA: Wiley.

Kuhnfeld, Megan, and Beth Tarasawa. 2020. "The COVID-19 Slide: What Summer Learning Loss Can Tell Us about the Potential Impact of School Closures on Student Academic Achievement." Retrieved June 12, 2020 (https://www.nwea.org/content/uploads/2020/05/Collaborative-Brief_Covid19-Slide-APR20.pdf).

Lemov, Doug. 2015. *Teach Like a Champion 2.0.* San Francisco, CA: Jossey-Bass.

Lenz, Bob. 2015. "Failure Is Essential to Learning." Retrieved March 31, 2022 (https://www.edutopia.org/blog/failure-essential-learning-bob-lenz).

List, John A. 2022. *The Voltage Effect: How to Make Good Ideas Great and Great Ideas Scale*. New York: Crown Publishing Group.

Marken, Alex, Jenny Scala, Marie Husby-Slater, and Garry Davis. 2020. *Early Warning Intervention and Monitoring System Implementation Guide*. AIR.

Marshall, Kim, and Dave Marshal. 2017. "Mini-Observations: A Keystone Habit." *School Administrator* 74(11):26–29.

Marshall, Maxine-Laurie. 2018. "The Symbiotic Relationship between Trust and Innovation." Retrieved May 20, 2020 (https://www.i-cio.com/big-thinkers/rachel-botsman/item/the-symbiotic-relationship-between-trust-and-innovation).

Meece, Judith L., Eric M. Anderman, and Lynley H. Anderman. 2006. "Classroom Goal Structure, Student Motivation, and Academic Achievement." *Annual Review of Psychology* 57(1):487–503.

Mehta, Jal, and Sarah Fine. 2019. *In Search of Deeper Learning: The Quest to Remake the American High School*. London: Harvard University Press.

Murdock-Perriera, Lisel Alice, and Quentin Sedlacek. 2018. "Questioning Pygmalion in the Twenty-First Century: The Formation, Transmission, and Attributional Influence of Teacher Expectancies." *Social Psychology of Education* 21(3):691–707.

Newport, Cal. 2021. *A World Without Email: Reimagining Work in an Age of Communication Overload*. New York: Penguin Publishing Group.

Paige, Mark, and Audrey Amrein. 2020. "'Houston, We Have a Lawsuit': A Cautionary Tale for the Implementation of Value-Added Models for High-Stakes Employment Decisions." *Educational Researcher* 49(5):335–59.

Palincsar, Annemarie, and Ann L. Brown. 1986. "Reciprocal Teaching of Comprehension-Fostering and Comprehension-Monitoring Activities." *Cognition and Instruction* 2:117–75.

Phillips, Owen. 2015. "Revolving Door of Teachers Costs Schools Billions Every Year." Retrieved April 23, 2020 (https://www.npr.org/sections/ed/2015/03/30/395322012/the-hidden-costs-of-teacher-turnover).

Porath, Christine. 2022. *Mastering Community: The Surprising Ways Coming Together Moves Us from Surviving to Thriving*. New York: Grand Central Publishing.

Porath, Christine, and Christine Pearson. 2013. "The Price of Incivility: Lack of Respect Hurts Morale—and the Bottom Line." *Harvard Business Review*:114–21.

Randolph, Justus J. 2007. "Meta-analysis of the research on response cards: Effects on test achievement, quiz achievement, participation, and off-task behavior." *Journal of Positive Behavior Interventions* 9(2):113–128.

Reeves, Douglas. 2013. *Finding Your Leadership Focus: What Matters Most for Student Results.* New York: Columbia University Teachers College Press.

Reeves, Douglas. 2018. "Seven Keys to Restoring the Teacher Pipeline." *Educational Leadership* 75(8).

Reeves, Douglas. 2020a. *Achieving Equity and Excellence: Immediate Results From the Lessons of High-Poverty, High-Success Schools.* Bloomington, IN: Solution Tree Press.

Reeves, Douglas. 2020b. "Supercharged Cabinet Meetings Establishing Norms, Recording Commitments and Requiring Evidence for the Body of Senior Leaders Who Advise the Superintendent." *School Administrator.*

Reeves, Douglas. 2020c. *The Learning Leader: How to Focus School Improvement for Better Results.* Alexandria, VA: Association for Supervision & Curriculum Development.

Reeves, Douglas. 2021a. *Deep Change Leadership: A Model for Renewing and Strengthening Schools and Districts.* Bloomington, IN: Solution Tree Press.

Reeves, Douglas. 2021b. *Fearless Schools: Building Trust and Resilience for Learning, Teaching, and Leading.* Boston, MA: Creative Leadership Press.

Reeves, Douglas. 2021c. *The Learning Leader: How to Focus School Improvement for Better Results.* 2nd ed. Alexandria, VA: Association for Supervision & Curriculum Development.

Reeves, Douglas, and Elle Allison. 2010. *Renewal Coaching Workbook.* San Francisco, CA: Jossey-Bass.

Reeves, Douglas, and Brooks Reeves. 2016. *The Myth of the Muse: Supporting Virtues That Inspire Creativity.* Bloomington, IN: Solution Tree Press.

Reeves, Douglas, and Robert Eaker. 2020. "A Comprehensive Guide to Overcoming the Effects of Fatigue in the Workplace." Retrieved May 7, 2020 (https://safestart.com/news/a-comprehensive-guide-to-overcoming-the-effects -of-fatigue-in-the-workplace/).

Rimm-Kaufma, Sara, and Lia Sandilos. 2010. "Improving Students' Relationships with Teachers to Provide Essential Supports for Learning." Retrieved February 21, 2022 (https://www.apa.org/education-career/k12/relationships).

Rogelberg, Steven G. 2019. *The Surprising Science of Meetings: How You Can Lead Your Team to Peak Performance.* London: Oxford University Press.

Rubie-Davies, Christine. 2014. *Becoming a High Expectation Teacher: Raising the Bar.* Hoboken, NJ: Routledge.

Rubie-Davies, Christine M., Elizabeth R. Peterson, Chris G. Sibley, and Robert Rosenthal. 2015. "A Teacher Expectation Intervention:

Modelling the Practices of High Expectation Teachers." *Contemporary Educational Psychology* 40:72–85.

Scherr, Rebecca. 2020. "The Conversation: Talking About Healthy Sexuality and Relationships." *Independent School* 80(1):110–12.

Schwartz, Barry. 2016. *The Paradox of Choice: Why More Is Less (Revised Edition)*. New York: HarperCollins Publishers.

Search Institute. 2018. *The Developmental Relationships Framework.* Minneapolis, MN.

Side by Side Educational Consulting. n.d. "20 active participation techniques to supercharge your lessons." (https://side bysideconsulting.com/wp-content/uploads/2017/10/20-Active_ Participation_Techniques_Handout.pdf).

Slavin, Robert. 2011. *Educational Psychology: Theory and Practice*. 10th ed. Boston, MA: Pearson.

Stephens-Davidowitz, Seth. 2017. *Everybody Lies: Big Data, New Data, and What the Internet Can Tell Us About Who We Really Are*. New York: Harper-Collins.

Tierny, John, and Roy Baumeister. 2019. *The Power of Bad: How the Negativity Effect Rules Us and How We Can Rule It*. New York: Penguin Press.

Tomlinson, Carol Ann. 2014. *The Differentiated Classroom: Responding to the Needs of all Learners*. 2nd ed. Alexandria, VA: ASCD.

Turkle, Sherry. 2016. *Reclaiming Conversation: The Power of Talk in a Digital Age*. New York: Penguin Publishing Group.

Vaughan, Winston. 2002. "Effects of Cooperative Learning on Achievement and Attitude Among Students of Color." *The Journal of Educational Research* 95(6):359–64.

Webb, Norman L. 1997. *Criteria for Alignment of Expectations and Assessments in Mathematics and Science Education* (Council of Chief State School Officers and National Institute for Science Education Research Monograph No. 6). Madison, WI: University of Wisconsin, Wisconsin Center for Education Research.

Welch, Jack. 2003. *Jack: Straight From the Gut*. New York: Grand Central Publishing.

Wood, Wendy. 2019. *Good Habits, Bad Habits: The Science of Making Positive Changes That Stick*. New York: Farrar, Straus and Giroux.

World Bank. 2021. "Learning Losses from COVID-19 Could Cost This Generation of Students Close to $17 Trillion in Lifetime Earnings." Retrieved February 12, 2022 (https://www.worldbank .org/en/news/press-release/2021/12/06/learning-losses-from-covid-19-could-cost-this-generation-of-students-close-to-17-tril lion-in-lifetime-earnings).

Zaleznik, Abraham. 1992. "Leaders and Managers: Are They Different?" *Harvard Business Review*, April.

Index

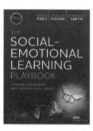

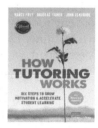

A SAGE Publishing Company

Helping educators make the greatest impact

CORWIN HAS ONE MISSION: to enhance education through intentional professional learning.

We build long-term relationships with our authors, educators, clients, and associations who partner with us to develop and continuously improve the best evidence-based practices that establish and support lifelong learning.